DANCER IN THE DARK

Lars von Trier

DANCER IN THE DARK

FILMFOUR 4

First published 2000 by FilmFour Books
an imprint of Macmillan Publishers Ltd
25 Eccleston Place, London SW1W 9NF
Basingstoke and Oxford

www.macmillan.com

Associated companies throughout the world.

ISBN 0 7522 1930 8

Text © Lars von Trier, 2000
Original lyrics © Lars von Trier & Sjón Sigurdsson

10 9 8 7 6 5 4 3

A CIP catalogue record for this book is available from the British Library.

Typeset by Blackjacks
Printed and bound in Great Britain by Mackays of Chatham, plc, Chatham, Kent.

Interview
with Lars von Trier

'It sounded so simple, to do a musical. It's an idea I'd always had. But who knows how to make a musical? I often try to go back to find the fascination I had as a child when I saw musicals on television, the ones with Gene Kelly. They were always very appealing and I thought that maybe I could recreate some of that feeling. I don't see musicals very often anymore but then, I saw them loads of times. Of course, my parents were communists and they thought that all musicals were American rubbish.

'I suppose that musicals are part of the family of melo-drama but the ones I saw as a child were never really danger-ous. You didn't cry. Musicals are like operettas; they're char-acterised by lightness. As a genre, they don't demand much of you – almost nothing. The first musicals I saw were very light. Then along came a fantastic one, *West Side Story* – that was more like a dramatic story.

'The difference between an opera and an operetta is that the heavy stuff is in the opera. *West Side Story* is more of an opera story than, say, *Singing in the Rain* where Debbie

Reynolds' drama is that she almost loses a career. It's normally smaller things that happen in a musical. What I wanted to achieve with *Dancer in the Dark* is that you take things as seriously as you do in an opera. Some years ago, people really cried at operas. I think it's a skill to be able to find such emotion in something so stylised. I would love to feel that much for someone who's been killed with a cardboard sword.

'I'm not particularly proud of the little tricks I've used for the musical numbers in *Dancer in the Dark*. I like the idea that Selma has these fantasies or this ability to hear music in everyday sounds, but I am not very proud that we didn't dare to make it cleaner and just allow them to sing for no reason. The problem is that when the music suddenly pours down from the sky, you have a tendency to do like they do in *The Muppet Show,* where everyone looks up to see where all the violins are located. That takes some of the pain and the danger away from the whole thing. I wanted the emotion and I wanted to communicate that emotion so we used this little trick and I hope it works.

'This film is put together from two 'shapes': the musical scenes and some almost documentary scenes. I thought it would be interesting to put the documentary style up against the musical but I believe that I act from admiration for the way musicals are – I'm not trying to subvert or destroy anything. I'm trying to make it richer by somehow importing true emotion. It is such a beautiful cocktail – emotion and music. Also, I think that to take something like musicals seriously is interesting. Gene Kelly did it to some degree and again, *West Side Story* did it. Most musicals exist only to entertain but I think they can contain so much more.

'The technique of using a hand-held camera and video has been extended to the musical scenes to keep the random effect – a 'live' quality. By using a lot of fixed cameras instead of staging a scene for one camera you should be able *not* to control the scene. You put up a lot of cameras and you get some gifts, in the same way you do when you work with a hand-held camera. If you want to bring the qualities of the 'looser' way of filmmaking we used in *Breaking the Waves* and *The Idiots* to the dance, I think this was the way to start. It's not perfected in any way; this was kind of a first stab at it but the 100 cameras enabled us to get shots that we wouldn't have had if we'd used a storyboard, some 'golden moments'. We actually could have used a lot more cameras – we had 100; we could have used 100 more. What the technique has proved is that it's a cheap way to achieve relatively high production values. In one scene, we danced for two days using 100 cameras. If we'd had one camera and a storyboard, it would have taken two weeks.

'Early on in my career if I had made a musical, I would have made it in a very traditional way with a lot of tracking shots and crane shots; it's logical; that's how to make image and music work together. But now, I have a tendency to put down rules for myself so I thought, 'No, let's go in the opposite direction and use only fixed cameras.' The idea was to get more gifts and to have less control. It's like a transmission or a live performance, not something filmed. If you watch a concert, somebody on a stage singing for example, you get closer because it hasn't been put together afterwards. Perhaps you can't see the difference, but you can *feel* it. In film, people have a tendency not to like direct transmission because they think it's like television or theatre. But the direction I have moved in for some time is actually more in that line. The best thing would have been if we could have done all of the song and dance numbers live and then lived with the mistakes. Björk had a very good idea in the beginning that the songs should be performed and recorded live but unfortunately we couldn't pull it off. The logistics of it turned out to be too difficult.

'The style of the music is the result of a collision between me and Björk. She's the one who knows about music and the film is about a woman who likes the same musicals as I liked back then. The biggest problem when you're making a musical is, of course, to decide what music you're going to put in and I had absolutely no idea. That's where Björk came in and I like the music she created very much. Some of it I had to learn to like but I did, very much, and it's a big part of the film. I couldn't have asked for a better performer in any way. The day before we started to shoot, I realised there was something I'd forgotten to do and that was to screen test Björk. But she gives an incredible performance and it's not acted, it's felt.

'This collision between cultures and people and different approaches is what makes films interesting. Catherine Deneuve hired herself – she wrote me a letter and asked if she could have a part and I said, 'Of course!' It seemed logical to offer her the part of Björk's 'partner', the other half of this very strange pair and I like them together. Although musicals are an American thing, there are some European ones and I knew the ones Catherine Deneuve starred in. To a degree, I was inspired by some of the scenes in those films.

'*Dancer in the Dark* is set in America because that's where musicals come from but also because it's a place I've never been to and will probably never visit because I don't go on aeroplanes. It's a kind of mythological country for me. We shot in Sweden and places that could look like America, and that may be more interesting than actually going to America. I'm always reminded of Kafka's *Amerika*. He had never been there and in the first pages of the novel, when he sails into the harbour of New York, he describes the Statue of Liberty carrying a big sword – I always thought that was quite poetic.

'I think that most people in Denmark find the death penalty very foreign. I'm not saying that Danish people are more humane than others, just that it's a tradition foreign to Scandinavians. Punishment altogether is illogical but I suppose you have to have punishments if a society is going to work. The death penalty doesn't seem like a punishment, however, it's more like revenge and it's dangerous to allow the state to have anything to do with revenge. I'm deeply against the death penalty. On the other hand, execution scenes are God's gift to directors. They're very efficient. If you're going to be a martyr you have to die.

'Selma's execution is a part of the melodrama – that and her blindness. There wasn't any blindness in the first script I sent to Björk but then I saw this beautiful cartoon, a Warner Brothers cartoon from the 1930s that was extremely cleverly done. A policeman in New York finds a doll and takes it to a woman he is in love with to give to her daughter. The little girl is sitting on the stairs playing with the doll and she drops it. When she goes to pick it up, she taps about on the ground without looking down – that's all you see and you understand that she's blind. It's extremely effective, very refined.

'The whole idea is that the little girl has never seen her mother, she's never seen the city and there are a lot of sounds around her. It's actually quite close to the story of *Dancer in the Dark*. The child imagines that the doll comes to life and takes her around to see all these things. She imagines that the sound of the subway is a roller-coaster and there are flowers everywhere which of course isn't true because it's actually a slum in New York. And then she imagines that she sees her mother. It's very melodramatic and very beautiful.

'I think that the more I work, the less my own person is involved. If you really work with a character, with an actor, it's as if you were making a documentary. You don't design something; you *investigate* something that is already there. Because it isn't my person and since it isn't only about things that happen in my twisted little brain, perhaps the work becomes more accessible.'

Reproduced with kind permission of Liz Miller/McDonald & Rutter

PRODUCED BY

Zentropa Entertainments4

Trust Film Svenska

Film i Väst

Liberator Productions

Written and directed by   Lars von Trier

Music composed by   Björk

Lyrics by   Lars von Trier & Sjón Sigurdsson

Still Photographers   David Koskas

Rolf Konow

CAST

Selma Jezková   Björk

Kathy   Catherine Deneuve

Bill   David Morse

Linda   Cara Seymour

Jeff   Peter Stormare

Norman   Jean-Marc Barr

Brenda   Siobhan Fallon

Oldrich Nový   Joel Grey

District Attorney   Željko Ivanek

Dr. Porkorný   Udo Kier

ADDITIONAL CAST

Morty   Jens Albinus

Judge   Reathel Bean

Receptionist   Mette Berggreen

Defense Attorney   Lars Michael Dinesen

Suzan   Katrine Falkenberg

Angry Man   Michael Flessas

Detective   John Randolph Jones

Officer of the Court   Noah Lazarus

Visitor   Sheldon Litt

Clerk of Court   Andrew Lucre

Chairman   John Martinus

New Defense Counsel   Luke Reilly

Boris   Tj Rizzo

Doctor   Stellan Skarsgård

Person in Doorway   Sean Michael Smith

Woman on Night Shift   Paprika Steen

Officer   Eric Voge

Man with Hood   Nick Wolf

Guard   Timm Zimmermann

CREW

Choreography & Dance Director   Vincent Paterson

Director of Photography   Robby Müller

Camera Operator   Lars von Trier

Casting by   Avy Kaufman

Casting UK   Joyce Nettles

Sound Designer   Per Streit

First Assistant Director   Anders Refn

Production Designer   Karl Juliusson

Art Director   Peter Grant

Costume Designer   Manon Rasmussen

Film Editors   Molly Malene Stensgaard

François Gedigier

Line Producer   Malte Forssell

Overture Sequence   Per Kirkeby

PRODUCERS

Produced by   Vibeke Windeløv

Executive Producer   Peter Aalbæk Jensen

Co-Executive Producers   Lars Jönsson

Marianne Slot

In co-production with   Pain Unlimited

Cinematograph

What Else?

Icelandic Film Corporation

France 3 Cinéma

Arte France Cinéma

The soundtrack to *Dancer in the Dark* is available
from One Little Indian, Polydor Records.

DANCER IN THE DARK

Screenplay by Lars von Trier

**Lyrics by Lars von Trier
& Sjón Sigurdsson**

OVERTURE

> *The theme from the 'Next-to-last-song'.*
> *It plays before the curtains are drawn.*

INT. REHEARSAL ROOM – DAY

> *SELMA and KATHY rehearse an amateur theater*
> *production. SELMA sings and dances to an*
> *upbeat piano accompaniment. She performs with*
> *naiveté and abandon, but with little talent. She is*
> *radiantly happy.*

SELMA   'Raindrops on roses and whiskers on kittens...'

> *KATHY dances on-stage carrying a paper rose*
> *and a toy cat. She shows them off as she dances.*
> *She is pretty good. She laughs and shakes her*
> *head. Exits quickly, reappears with new items:*
> *an old kettle and a pair of mittens.*

SELMA   'Bright copper kettles and warm woolen mittens...'

KATHY   *(to SELMA)* It's really no good…

> *SELMA creases up with laughter. KATHY brings in*
> *an armful of paper sacks.*

SELMA   *(pronouncing with difficulty)* 'Brown paper
            packages tied up with strings.'

KATHY   *(to SELMA, laughing)* It's impossible. I'm too old for this.

SELMA   *(to KATHY)* Hey, it's going fantastic. Listen to your heart, Kathy! 'These are a few of my favorite things.'

           KATHY rushes off in a fumble and brings back everything at once.

SELMA   *(stumbling with lyrics, giggling)* 'Cream colored ponies and crisp apple strudels. Doorbells and sleighbells and schnitzel with noodles. Wild geese that fly with the moon on their wings, these are a few of my favorite things.'

           KATHY exits, shaking her head. SELMA can do no more; she falls over and laughs. BORIS and SAMUEL watch. SAMUEL's eyes are wet with laughter. He wipes away his tears. BORIS is not laughing.

BORIS   You sure you think she's good enough for the part? Her singing's very strange, and she can't dance.

SAMUEL   Oh, come on, it's the first time she's tried it. She just has a particular way of approaching the song. Sure, it's not perfect, but Selma has everything our Maria needs. She's a natural.

SAMUEL blows his nose, goes on laughing.

*At the end of the music, SELMA does a
tap-shuffle on her way off stage.*

SAMUEL *(in earnest)* No, no, Selma... I told you...
There is no tapping in *Sound of Music*!

SELMA *(pleading)* Come on, Samuel...just a little...
It IS a musical, right?

KATHY walks up to SELMA smiling.

KATHY What a mess! I'm not a dancer!

SELMA No, no, we looked like a million dollars!
We're amateurs, and that's the way it should be.
Listen to your heart, that's all that matters...
(mischievously) Cvalda!

KATHY Don't call me that! You know I don't want you to
call me that!

BORIS is still observing them.

BORIS She's got glasses! If I'm playing Von Trapp,
I'm not sure Maria should have glasses.

SAMUEL You're so young. Can't you see what kind of
Maria we've got here? No, we'll never improve on
her, spectacles or no spectacles.

SAMUEL smiles to SELMA and KATHY.

SELMA   *(to SAMUEL)* It's hard to dance when there's no rhythm. Can't we find somebody to play drums?

SAMUEL   *(smiles at her)* That's a good idea. We'll look into that.

INT. DOCTOR'S EXAMINATION ROOM/ BATHROOM – DAY

> *SELMA, in the bathroom, takes a large sheet of paper from her shoulder bag, unfolds it. It is covered in rows of big letters and numbers. She studies it and memorizes it.*

INT. DOCTOR'S EXAMINATION ROOM – DAY

> *KATHY and the DOCTOR wait. SELMA enters.*

DOCTOR Are you ready now?

SELMA   Yes, I am ready.

> *The DOCTOR points at his chart. SELMA calls out the numbers and letters he indicates.*

DOCTOR Well, well, well. That's fine, Mrs. Jezková, your eyes seem to be doing all right. I see no reason why you shouldn't go on working at that machine of yours. I'll write to the plant and let them know.

SELMA smiles to KATHY, who smiles back in relief. They leave.

EXT. STREET WITH SHOPS – DAY

SELMA and KATHY are window-shopping. They pass a jewelry store.

SELMA   A Cvalda is a big and happy one. You're so serious always, Kathy. And yet deep down inside – you are a Cvalda, I know it. Big and happy.

KATHY   Hey, come on! I'm not big!

SELMA   No, but inside. Being a bit more happy wouldn't hurt you.

Something occurs to SELMA. She pulls KATHY through the doorway into the shop. KATHY resists; she doesn't want to enter the expensive store.

INT. JEWELRY STORE – DAY

SELMA tugs KATHY to the counter. The SHOP ASSISTANT scrutinizes them.

SELMA   *(smiles)* Hello! We are Von Trapps. We wish to see
          the biggest ruby in your store.

SHOP ASSISTANT
          The Von Trapps?

SELMA   Yes, I'm Selma and this is Cvalda! I am very
          interested in precious stones. They become me,
          my admirers tell me – what do you think?

SHOP ASSISTANT
          Well, I guess—

          *He unlocks a glass case and brings out a tray of
          rubies.*

SELMA   Is that all you have? I imagined something much
          bigger. Perhaps a necklace or a ring with a big
          stone—

SHOP ASSISTANT
          I can obtain something like that – if you are
          interested, Ma'am.

SELMA   *(winks to Kathy)* I am indeed! Let me have the
          necklace and the ring and – a bracelet – but
          make sure it has seven stones; I have seven
          children… by marriage that is.

          *KATHY is beside herself. SELMA winks at her.
          The SHOP ASSISTANT finds some forms.*

SHOP ASSISTANT
>Who shall I contact when your purchases arrive?

SELMA   Don't worry about that! I'll drop in again.

INT. BUS – DAY

>*KATHY is furious. SELMA is laughing.*
>*They are on the bus.*

KATHY   I'm not shopping with you if you're going to act
>like a clown. You've got to behave yourself. Now
>he's going to buy all that stuff!

SELMA   *(rummages in her shoulder bag)* Sure, sure. It was
>only a bit of fun. He'll sell it to somebody. People
>are so rich in America! And it was just for a laugh
>– Cvalda!

>*SELMA extracts a little pile of cards and a handful*
>*of hairpins. She hands them to KATHY.*

KATHY   I won't help you with these if you're going to be
>such a pain.

SELMA   *(wheedling)* Oh—

KATHY   No, I mean it. You'll just have to do your silly old
>hairpins by yourself.

SELMA   Really? Well lucky old me – I can do just that.

SELMA slips pins into the holes in the card at a blazing pace. KATHY watches her for a while. Then, with a sigh, she takes more cards and needles out of SELMA's shoulder bag. Slowly she starts working away.

KATHY   I sure hope your pop appreciates all the money you send him. Or I'd feel idiotic doing all these hairpins.

SELMA   *(smiles)* Oh, he does. Don't you worry!

INT. FACTORY – DAY

SELMA and KATHY are toiling amidst the polyrhythmic acoustic inferno.

KATHY is on a similar machine further back. Now and then, SELMA glances at the script in her shoulder bag. She needs to look at it pretty closely.

SELMA is working an enormous press that presses out stainless steel sinks. She lubricates a steel plate with soap-water, then she fits the plate into the press, which shapes it into a sink. She hands the sink to a YOUNG BOY standing next to her, who cuts the edges of the sinks with a big

*pair of plate-scissors. All around her PEOPLE
work with sinks. Now and then other WORKERS
deliver her plates and soap-water.*

SELMA *(to herself, does not understand)* 'So long,
farewell, auf wiedersehn, adieu. Adieu, adieu,
to yieu and yieu and yieu…'

*SELMA mouths the lines again. She has trouble
with the 'yieu!' She looks at the noisy machine
inferno. The noise pulses rhythmically through the
hall. She smiles and disappears into her own
thoughts. KATHY looks across at her in concern.*

*By mistake, SELMA almost drops a plate as
she soaps it in.*

*NORMAN walks past. He looks at her
admonishingly. She smiles back.*

NORMAN You can't bring that script to work. Learn your
lines in your own time. Keep your eyes on the
machine. Last night we had to stop for five hours,
because some idiot broke a tool…

SELMA Sure, sure—

KATHY If you'd quit interrupting us, Norman, it would be
less dangerous to your machines.

9

NORMAN *(hesitantly)* I came to tell Selma that Bill's here –
with Gene.

*SELMA comes back to earth. She looks livid.
She leaves the machine as it presses out a new
sink. NORMAN takes over the machine.*

SELMA strides out.

SELMA   Damn it, Gene! That does it!

KATHY   Take it easy, Selma...

*KATHY runs after SELMA. NORMAN, taking over
KATHY's machine as well, yells after them.*

NORMAN You gotta come right back, you hear?

*NORMAN runs from machine to machine, doing a
little of both women's jobs.*

EXT. FACTORY – DAY

*A police car waits outside the factory. BILL stands
beside the open car door in his cop's uniform. He
watches SELMA as she rushes towards the car.
She hauls GENE out of the back seat. She whips
his glasses off and gives him three mighty slaps.
KATHY and BILL try to stop her.*

SELMA   Do prdele Evzên. Can't you get it into your head
          that when I say you go to school you go to
          school!

          She tears herself away from KATHY and BILL,
          and slaps him again.

SELMA   You think I joke? When I say you got to study you
          got to study – and not hang out with that gang of
          automobile thieves—

GENE   I don't wanna go to that dumb school.

SELMA   You'll go just as long as I say you've got to go!

KATHY   Selma! Easy does it! That'll do!

SELMA   No it won't – he must go to school!

KATHY   He'll learn what he has to in due time…

SELMA   I'll decide that, thank you.

          GENE is crying.

SELMA   And stop crying for Christ's sake. Stop feeling so
          goddamn sorry for yourself!

          JEFF pulls up in his pickup. He opens the door
          and steps down. He looks at SELMA.

JEFF   Should I run him on over to school, Selma?

          SELMA turns angrily to JEFF.

SELMA   Is it your business, all of a sudden? What're you
          doing here at all? Come by to pick me up or
          something?

JEFF   *(shyly)* I came by to ask if I could drive you home—

SELMA   *(angrily)* But I don't punch out for another two
          hours.

JEFF   Sometimes you punch out early.

SELMA   I never punch out early!

JEFF   Well, if you don't want a ride...

SELMA   No I damned well don't!

          *She turns on her heel and stalks angrily inside.
          They all watch her go. BILL eases GENE into the
          back of the police car again.*

BILL   OK, Mr. G. I'd better run you up to school...

EXT. FACTORY – EVENING

          The factory horn sounds. WORKERS emerge.

12

SELMA and KATHY come out together.

JEFF sidles up behind them.

JEFF *(quietly)* If you've changed your mind, Selma,
      I'd be happy to run you home—

SELMA No thank you! I have my bicycle.

      SELMA gets her bike out of a storage space.
      A freight train passes.

KATHY *(looks at Jeff)* She likes you, I'm sure of it.

JEFF You are?

INT. TRAILER – EVENING

      SELMA practices tap dancing on a wooden
      board in the living area, to the beat of an old
      metronome. GENE is hunched over his supper,
      the open script beside him. Still putting pins into
      cardboard, SELMA tries a fancy dance step, but
      can't get it right.

SELMA 'So long, farewell, auf wiedersehn, adieu. Adieu,
      adieu to yieu and yieu and yieu…'

      SELMA looks uncertainly at GENE. He looks
      down at the lines in the script.

GENE   That's what it says…

SELMA   But what does it mean? 'Yieu and yieu and yieu?'

GENE   How should I know? It's your dumb musical!

SELMA   You seem to think everything's dumb—

GENE   The others say you can't dance. How long do I
         have to read this for you?

SELMA   You'll finish when I say so and not before. It is
         your punishment for not going to school. And eat
         up when I cook for you!

         *GENE prods at his supper. She looks at him
         affectionately.*

SELMA   Are you tired, my pet?

         GENE snarls.

GENE   Oh, cut it out, Mom, okay?

SELMA   I just think you look tired.

         GENE doesn't reply.

SELMA   For God's sake! I was only asking.

A knock on the door. SELMA answers, it's
LINDA. She steps into the trailer.

LINDA   You want to come over to our place and listen to
        some music?

SELMA   *(smiles)* It's kind of you, but there's really no
        need…

        LINDA bends down to GENE.

LINDA   You fancy comin' down to me and Bill's place?

SELMA   *(pulling her coat on)* Don't bother to ask him.
        He's just cross.

EXT. BILL AND LINDA'S HOUSE – EVENING

        SELMA and GENE emerge from the trailer,
        accompanied by LINDA. Crossing Bill and Linda's
        garden, they head for the house. BILL waits in the
        doorway. SELMA whispers to GENE.

SELMA   Ask Bill about his money. Linda likes us to talk
        about it.

        GENE looks angry.

INT. BILL AND LINDA'S HOUSE – EVENING

> *SELMA sits at the table, looking around LINDA and BILL's home. BILL enters, carrying a gramophone, and puts on some easy-listening classical music. BILL and LINDA start sticking hairpins into cards. They put the finished cards into SELMA's shoulder bag. GENE is on the couch, looking angry and bored. LINDA walks up to the table with a candy tin.*

SELMA   *(smiling)* You have such a beautiful home!

LINDA   *(smiles)* That's what I'm always telling Bill.

BILL   *(smiles)* Oh, it's nothing, really.

LINDA   Sure it is. I don't reckon anybody would expect your average police officer to have a place like this!

> *She smiles at BILL, who looks bashful.*

BILL   Linda's great at making things look spiffy.

SELMA   Yes, and of course, there's all that money you inherited, Bill—

> *LINDA smiles and nods. SELMA looks at her. Then at BILL.*

16

SELMA   Where do you keep it? In the bank?

LINDA   In a safe deposit box. Right, Bill? Bill thinks it's
         for the best.

SELMA   *(smiles affably)* Oh, a safe deposit box!
         Good thing you don't keep it here. It wouldn't
         be very safe – though it might be kind of nice,
         too, 'cause then you could look at it once in
         a while.

LINDA   Sometimes Bill brings the box home, to check
         on things – accounts and stuff – you do, don't
         you, Bill? But I guess nobody'd mess with a
         police officer.

         BILL nods and shrugs his shoulders.
         SELMA smiles at LINDA, who looks contented.
         LINDA offers the tin round. It's 'Almond Roca'.
         SELMA's eyes light up at the sight of the tin.

SELMA   You always give us such fine and expensive
         things when we come to see you.

BILL   Oh, Linda has always appreciated the good
         things.

SELMA   I once saw a movie. Back home in
         Czechoslovakia. They were eating candy from a
         tin like this. I thought, 'How wonderful it must be
         in the United States.'

LINDA   (smiles) I guess it was a musical, right?

SELMA smiles and nods. She eats the candy solemnly. GENE gobbles his. LINDA sits down and cards a few hairpins.

SELMA   Thank you for helping today, Bill. You're such a kind officer!

LINDA   Yes, and you know why, it's because he doesn't have to be one. He wouldn't work if he didn't want to. He's not in it for the money. He just plain likes helping folks.

BILL   Well, work does a body good.

LINDA   But I'm right? Right, Bill? You don't actually need the job?

BILL   All right, all right – let's just say so.
(he starts to clear the table and wipes it off with a cloth) Whyn't you drop Mr. G. off here tomorrow before you go to work? Linda will make sure he gets to school on time, won't you, Linda? That way Selma will know that young Wildeye's at school and not getting himself into trouble.

LINDA   Why, hon, that's a terrific idea—

SELMA smiles as she looks around the neat, tidy home.

EXT. BILL AND LINDA'S HOUSE – EVENING

> *GENE and SELMA are about to return to the trailer. Behind them, LINDA reopens the door. She holds out the candy tin. She puts a finger to her lips.*

LINDA   *(whispers)* Take the rest with you. Bill will never notice.

SELMA   Oh, it's too much!

> *LINDA smiles and offers the tin.*

LINDA   Oh, go on!

> *LINDA gives SELMA a kiss on the cheek and goes inside. SELMA stands there for a moment, looking at the tin, dreaming.*

INT. TRAILER – NIGHT

> *SELMA empties the last few candies from the tin. She unwraps the wax paper from one of them, smells it and looks at it. Then she rewraps it diligently. She wraps the remaining candies in a piece of paper and puts them into a bag hanging on the wall.*

Glancing across to GENE's room to make sure he is asleep, she steps over to a loose panel in the wall. She eases it open and retrieves a large envelope stuffed with dollar bills all neatly folded with rubber bands around them.

She throws the envelope away and puts the money into the candy tin instead. She looks at the tin, a smile on her lips, and replaces it behind the panel.

EXT. BILL AND LINDA'S HOUSE – MORNING

SELMA knocks on the door. She has GENE with her. She holds a wooden box and the bag containing the taffies. GENE shivers a bit, unused to being up so early. LINDA answers the door.

SELMA   (smiles) It's the first of the month!

SELMA hands some dollar bills to LINDA. LINDA accepts them without counting them.

LINDA   You always pay right on time. Hi there, Gene.

SELMA   Everything in its place. Now, about Gene...

LINDA   Yes, that's right! Come on in, Gene! Don't worry, I'll get him off to school okay.

SELMA   Thank you.

SELMA hands GENE his bag, knowing he'll be delighted when he finds the taffies inside.

INT. FACTORY LOCKER ROOM – MORNING

SELMA wears her smock. She picks up the wooden box and walks over to MORTY, who sits on a bench, changing into work clothes. She hands him the box. He opens it and peers inside. He closes it.

MORTY   Want another?

SELMA   Sure.

MORTY   A big 'un or a little 'un?

SELMA   How many's a 'big 'un?'

MORTY   A big 'un'd be 10,000.

SELMA   I'll take a 'big 'un'.

MORTY looks into his locker. He selects a box from among many that are there. He gives it to SELMA and puts the one she has just given him on a shelf. Then he pulls out his wallet and gives her two bills, clipped to a small blue receipt. She takes them and folds them neatly.

INT. FACTORY – DAY

KATHY and SELMA are on their break. SELMA cards pins, reads her script, while KATHY drinks coffee and reads a magazine. NORMAN enters.

NORMAN   Can you do a couple hours' overtime again tonight, Selma?

SELMA looks up. KATHY interrupts.

KATHY   No, she can't. Not tonight. We're going to catch a movie.

SELMA   Maybe we could see it tomorrow?

KATHY   No. Tonight's musical night!

SELMA smiles. She listens to the sound of the factory, and for a second or two the noise becomes music, the WORKERS moving to the music.

INT. FACTORY – DAY

Song: 'Cvalda'

INT. CINEMA – NIGHT

> *KATHY and SELMA watch a musical. It's* Top Hat *with Fred Astaire and Ginger Rodgers. They are sitting in the pavilion in the rain and Fred has just sung.*

KATHY   *(whispers)* Now he gets up. It's still raining.

SELMA   *(whispers in irritation)* I know it is… are they good friends now?

KATHY   It doesn't look like it. Well, she gets up too…

> *A MAN beside them shushes them.*

KATHY   Hey, give us a break! Just because her eyes aren't so good…

ANGRY MAN
> I paid good money to see this movie…

KATHY   So did she.
(to SELMA)
They're dancing now…

ANGRY MAN
> It's a goddamned musical, of course they're dancing!

> *SELMA looks up at the screen with a smile as the music thunders out over her.*

INT. TRAILER – NIGHT

> *BILL, KATHY and LINDA come up to the trailer door. They have sly smiles on their faces. SELMA opens the door.*

SELMA   Hello?

LINDA   Hi, Selma...

> *SELMA looks suspicious. They come in and sit down. GENE looks out from his room, curious.*

SELMA   *(looks at KATHY)* You've come to tell me something?

KATHY   *(pretending not to care)* No... no...

BILL   Selma...

SELMA   Yes?

BILL   It's about the bike...

> *SELMA gets up. Now she understands. She shakes her head.*

SELMA   No bike! When I was a child I walked. Gene can walk.

BILL	But he says he could make it to school in time on his own if he had a bike…
SELMA	*(angry now)* So that's what he says? *(turns to GENE)* You asked them to come here?
GENE	No!
SELMA	Well you can all save your trouble… I will not buy Gene a bike.
GENE	I'm almost the only kid in my class who doesn't have a bike. I know a boy who got a scooter!
SELMA	You know very well I don't have any money. Every time I make ten bucks I send them to grandad and the folks back home. The money does more good there.
GENE	Grandad!
KATHY	But Selma…
SELMA	*(angrily)* No, he's got to get it into his head – and all of you for that matter – I will not spend the money on expensive presents for him – and not even when it's his birthday… that's the kind of mom he has for himself. I'm sure he'd rather have another—
KATHY	*(to GENE, smiles)* Your mother is only teasing. Look what she has brought for you.

She looks conspiratorial. She points through the window. GENE looks. SELMA doesn't understand. JEFF appears outside, pulling a bike. He displays it.

GENE   *(looks at Selma)* A bike!

SELMA   It is not from me, and you all know it!
        (turns to the others)
        We can't accept.

KATHY   It's secondhand. Bill picked it up at work – Jeff fixed it up – it isn't worth that many of your precious dollars.

SELMA   Thank you very much, but in my family we buy what we need.

GENE   Oh, Mom!

KATHY   Well, there's nowhere for us to take it back to. And even if it costs us our friendship, Gene is going to have that bicycle. Just like all the other kids.

        SELMA is about to speak. But then she looks at GENE, who looks beseechingly at her. KATHY looks firmly at SELMA. SELMA reconsiders. She gives in.

SELMA   If you promise to go to school – and get there on time and do all your assignments and read at

least one book for every time you ride your bike
I suppose we'll be able to pay for it one day.

GENE   *(happy)* I promise!

          SELMA smiles reluctantly. The others are also
          smiling now. LINDA brings in some fruit juice and
          JEFF brings in the bike. He shows it off to GENE.

JEFF   It's not exactly a scooter...

BILL   *(cheerfully)* Maybe it is... Mr. G.

          BILL shows them the bit of wood he's wedged
          into the front wheel; when GENE rides the bike,
          it sounds like a scooter. GENE rides noisily out
          the door and round and round the trailer. He is
          delighted. SELMA watches him through the
          window, smiling.

INT. TRAILER – NIGHT

          SELMA watches GENE sleep. His glasses rest on
          the bedside table, his new bike leans against his
          bed. SELMA exits, closes the door behind her.
          She tidies up a bit and starts carding. She also
          starts the metronome. She smiles as she listens.
          There is a soft knock at the door. She answers it.
          It is BILL. He looks a bit distracted.

SELMA   Bill – something up?

BILL   No, no, I couldn't sleep, that's all.

         SELMA stops the metronome and pours BILL
         a cup of coffee. He sits there for a long time
         without a word. She looks at him, and he starts
         to cry. She takes his hand gravely.

BILL   Can I tell you, Selma?

SELMA   Yes, you can.

BILL   I have no money.

         He looks at her desperately.

BILL   The money I inherited is long since gone. Linda
         spends and spends and well, my salary is
         nowhere near enough. I can't say no to her.
         And now they are going to repossess the house
         because I can't keep up the payments. Linda will
         never get over it... I know she won't... I know
         she won't...

         He cries a little. She looks at him sympathetically.
         He pulls himself together.

BILL   I'm glad I've told someone. I feel much better
         now. And I know I can trust you not to breathe a
         word to anyone.

*She nods. His hand shakes as he drinks some
more of the coffee. He looks at her.*

BILL Now you know my secret, Selma.

*SELMA nods. Her gaze grows distant. There is a
moment's silence. She looks at him.*

SELMA I also have a secret that nobody knows.

BILL looks at her quietly.

SELMA I am going blind. I'm not blind yet, but soon,
maybe even sometime this year...

*She smiles to herself. She looks at BILL,
who is aghast.*

SELMA Oh, it's not as bad as it sounds... I've always
known it would happen. It's a family thing. That's
why I came to America. Because in America they
can give Gene an operation.

She sits there a moment.

SELMA He will have his operation when he is 13. They
told me not to tell him beforehand. That can
make it worse. I almost have the money now.

BILL So you made up that story about sending money
to your dad?

SELMA   *(shakes her head)* I never knew my dad.

BILL   That's why you put in all those hours. You've
        been saving up to pay for Gene's operation?

SELMA   Well, it's my fault.

BILL   How come?

SELMA   I knew he would have the same bad eyes as me,
        but I had him all the same.

        *BILL looks at her. She is quite relaxed, and she
        nods a little to herself.*

SELMA   But now I have saved up almost enough money.
        I must hurry and get the rest before my own
        eyes go.

        BILL looks at her sympathetically.

BILL   You are strong, Selma. Very strong!

        SELMA shakes her head.

SELMA   When I hear the machines at the factory I can't
        stop myself from dreaming that it is music – I
        don't need an orchestra, just a few noises, and
        then, the music comes. *(switches on metronome
        and dreams a little)* It's the kind of thing that
        worsens when you can't see very well—

BILL looks at her, listening. SELMA giggles.

SELMA   I just hate it when the songs in the movies get
         real big, with whole crowds of people and stuff,
         and the camera goes through the roof – because
         then it's the last song, and that will be that. When
         I was a child I always left after the next to last
         song… so it never stopped…

         They sit there awhile.

BILL   Thanks for telling me your secret. Now we know
         something about each other. I'm sure you'll fix
         Gene up. Maybe they'll even fix you up, too.

SELMA   *(smiles)* Oh, I doubt it—

         *BILL gets up to go. SELMA opens the door
         for him.*

SELMA   Bill!

         He turns around at the foot of the short steps.

SELMA   I'm sure you'll puzzle out how to keep your home.

BILL   Yeah, I guess I just might. Goodnight, Selma.

SELMA   Goodnight, Bill.

         BILL walks off. Then he turns around.

BILL   Selma, mum's the word, right?

SELMA   Mum?

BILL   We don't tell anybody...

SELMA   Right, Bill – I promise—

She stands there a while and watches him go before she closes her door. BILL heads towards his house. From behind a curtain LINDA watches him. As he approaches, she moves away so as not to be spotted.

EXT. TRAILER – MORNING

SELMA gets out her bike. She pushes it towards the street, but, squinting out at the morning traffic, she's overtaken by doubt. She puts it back. Behind the house a train loaded with woods passes. She watches it.

INT. FACTORY – DAY

NORMAN, SELMA and KATHY are on their break. They sip coffee as they card pins.

NORMAN What's his name, anyhow?

SELMA   Whose?

NORMAN Your old man – isn't he the one we're carding all
       these everlovin' pins for?

KATHY   His name is Oldrich Nový and he lives outside
         Prague. In the country on a big lake.

NORMAN But you are not called Nový, Selma...

SELMA   *(brushes it aside, somewhat discomforted)*
         Hey, you needn't do any more if you don't want,
         I can manage on my own.

NORMAN *(with irony)* I thought commies made a big deal
       out of sharing everything...

SELMA   They do, and it's a fine thing... they're just poor.

NORMAN What are you doing here then, if you think
       Czechoslovakia is so much better than the
       US of A?

SELMA   *(defiantly)* Maybe Czechoslovakia is better for
         people...

         *SELMA gets up. She puts the finished card into
         her shoulder bag and heads for the door. She
         turns with a smile.*

SELMA   But the doctors are better in the US of A!

NORMAN watches her return to her machine.
She takes over from the person who has been
standing in for her. After a while she starts gazing
dreamily across the machines. Their rhythm is
massive now. She gazes at all the moving parts.
Slowly the rhythm turns into music.

INT. FACTORY – DAY

Song: 'Cvalda'

SELMA smiles and closes her eyes. For an instant
the music comes back. A WORKER dances up to
her. He walks around her with his hands in his
pockets as Fred Astaire did in Top Hat. Others do
small steps in the background.

INT. FACTORY – DAY

Selma wakes up and smiles.

INT. FACTORY – DAY

NORMAN and KATHY still sit at the table.
KATHY still cards hairpins. NORMAN looks at her.
She looks up at him.

KATHY   Just be grateful you don't live in Czechoslovakia.
         There are people starving there.

NORMAN There are people starving here!

KATHY   Not if they're prepared to roll up their sleeves!

NORMAN Maybe.

         He gets up and goes into the other hall.
         KATHY finishes the card and pops it into
         SELMA's shoulder bag. As she does so, she
         finds the folded chart. She gets it out, unfolds it.
         KATHY looks at the letters and numbers in
         shock. Shaking her head, she looks out at
         SELMA, who is dreaming away at her machine.

         She sees that SELMA is carelessly about to start
         the machine with a new plate in it, without taking
         the sink she made before out first. She runs
         towards her.

INT. FACTORY – DAY

         KATHY comes up to SELMA's machine and stops
         SELMA from starting the machine with the two
         plates in it. SELMA wakes up and quickly gets the
         second plate out of the way. But NORMAN's not
         fooled. He shakes his head.

NORMAN You know what happens if you just put a new plate in don't you? If you don't take the old one out first?

KATHY Yes, yes... but she didn't...

NORMAN You destroy the tool... it takes a whole day to mend it. Never two plates, Selma... Never!!! Always remove the sink you just made first. Always!!

NORMAN shows how you can see that there is still a sink in the machine.

KATHY *(with assumed jocularity)* Sure, sure, Norman – we all know that. Just take it easy, okay?

NORMAN leaves, still serious. KATHY gives SELMA an angry look and goes to her own machine. SELMA goes on working.

EXT. FACTORY – EVENING

SELMA and KATHY emerge from the factory. KATHY is angry.

KATHY You cheated the doctor! You shouldn't be working at the press at all! How dare you! Just how much can you see?

SELMA Oh stop it! I could work it with my eyes closed.

You could too. Just because I can't see those
dumb letters doesn't mean I can't do my work.
It was only because I started dreaming.

KATHY   Dreaming! About what?

SELMA   That there was music and we were all
dancing... don't you hear the music the
machines make?

KATHY   No, but then I'm not a real American. Not the way
you are.

SELMA   *(astonished)* Am I a real American?

KATHY   *(nods)* That's exactly what you are. You dream
like an American, but I don't. I know that a
machine is a machine, and when it makes a noise
it is not making music or tap-dancing its way
through a movie. When it makes a noise, it's to
keep you awake and on your toes. Because it's
not just that you can break the machine, but also,
it can cut off your hands just like that... You have
to watch out every second. Promise me you'll
stay awake, okay?

SELMA   *(smiles)* Yes, I promise to stay awake!

KATHY   *(looks at her earnestly)* You've got to listen to
what I'm saying, Selma. Seriously.

SELMA   I know it, I know it. I promise I won't dream any
         more. I'll keep my eyes open.

KATHY   Good!

         KATHY leaves. JEFF walks up to SELMA.
         They watch KATHY go.

JEFF   If you're not going with Kathy, can I give you
         a lift home?

SELMA   No, I don't want a boyfriend, I've told you that...
         You're a nice guy Jeff, but I don't have time for a
         boyfriend. Not right now.

JEFF   All I'm asking is drive you on home. I can throw
         your bike in back.

SELMA   If I wanted a boyfriend it would be you, that's for
         sure. But I don't want one. Not now.

         SELMA picks up her bike. He puts his hand on it.

JEFF   You know, it's not really safe for you to ride that
         bike, what with you – er – wearin' glasses and all.

SELMA   *(pulling out into the street)*
         No need for you to worry.

         Just as she speaks SELMA almost cycles into a
         huge truck. It brakes and sounds its horn. She

shakes her fist at it, but remains rooted to the
spot, trembling, as the truck drives off.

SELMA   (noticing JEFF watching her, shouts)
         No need for you to distract me like that, either.

         JEFF looks down. He crosses to his pick-up
         and drives off. SELMA watches him go.
         Now BILL comes by in his police car.
         He gives SELMA a wave.

INT. POLICE CAR – EVENING

         SELMA is in the car, which idles near a small yard
         near the tracks. The bike pokes out of the trunk.
         SELMA looks sympathetically at BILL.

SELMA   How did it go today?

         BILL doesn't reply. He looks at her, then looks
         away again.

BILL   If I could make the next payment I'd have a bit
         more time...

SELMA   (consolatory) Yes, and then you'd figure a
         way out for sure...

         BILL turns and looks her in the eye.

BILL   All I need is a loan, just for a month or so—

            *SELMA understands what he's driving at. She sits
            there awkwardly. Gazing through the windshield,
            she shakes her head.*

SELMA   I can't do that, Bill. I'm sorry—

BILL   *(beseeching)* Just for a month. After all,
            Gene has no idea you've been saving up.
            And in a month, he won't even be 13 yet… Linda
            had nothing when she was a kid – that's why our
            home means so much to her—

SELMA   No, Bill. I can't. That money belongs to Gene.
            I don't dare lend it to you… I promise him the
            operation every single night after he falls asleep.
            No, Bill, it's impossible.

            *BILL sits awhile in silence. He has humiliated
            himself by asking. For a second we can see he is
            hurt. He smiles apologetically.*

BILL   I should never have asked—

SELMA   Hey, of course you should. No harm in asking.
            I just can't do it, that's all—

BILL   How can I allow myself to ask such a thing?
            How dumb can a guy get? It's unforgivable.

SELMA   *(pleading)* Bill! I'm just as sorry as you are, but I
           don't dare do anything right now. I won't be able
           to keep my job much longer, the way things are –
           I still haven't got all the money I need, and my
           eyes are going fast – I can't even ride my bike
           home any more.

BILL   *(hardly hears her)* I'm sure things'll work out for
           both of us, Selma. I'm just under so much
           pressure. I guess I could try talking to the Savings
           and Loan again. Linda wants new couches—

           BILL starts the car again. He turns to SELMA.

BILL   *(with a crooked smile)* I can always shoot myself.
           That'd probably be the easiest—

SELMA   Bill! You mustn't say things like that!

BILL   No, no. Just kidding.

           BILL pulls out onto the road.

INT./EXT. TRAILER – EARLY MORNING

           *SELMA lies awake in bed. She hears a door open
           down at the house. She looks into the garden.
           BILL walks towards the mobile home. He stands
           there awhile, unable to make up his mind whether
           or not to come in. He turns and goes back inside*

41

*his house. He does not spot SELMA. She lies
down again. Back at the house LINDA also steps
away from the window. SELMA is still lying there,
awake, gazing at the ceiling, when her alarm clock
goes off.*

INT./EXT. BILL AND LINDA'S HOUSE – MORNING

*SELMA drops GENE off at LINDA's. BILL is there,
too. He avoids SELMA's eye.*

SELMA   Can I pay you something for minding Gene and
        taking him to school? After all, you are not
        obligated to do it. And maybe the rent I pay you
        is way too low, with the way everything else
        keeps going up—

LINDA   No, Selma, you keep your money. You need it
        more than we do.

        *SELMA looks at BILL, who lowers his gaze.
        LINDA hands him his lunch tin and thermos. He
        emerges from the study, carrying his service
        pistol. He is in uniform, but without his belt. He
        hurries out. LINDA looks at him coldly as he goes.*

        *SELMA glances outside. She sees BILL pick up
        his belt from inside the car and put it on. He
        pushes the gun into its holster. He comes back in
        and goes to his room.*

SELMA   Does he bring his gun into your home?

LINDA   Why of course he does, Selma. He's a police
         officer. He has to bring it home. But he keeps it
         locked up in his desk drawer, no need to fret.

SELMA   *(apologizing for her ignorance)*
         I just had no idea he kept it at home.

         *SELMA gives GENE a kiss and his bag; he shies
         away; she leaves.*

EXT. TRAILER – MORNING

         *SELMA gets on her bike. The wooden box of pins
         is on the luggage rack. She is about to set off, but
         suddenly her courage fails her. She looks up at
         the railroad line. A freight train is passing. She
         takes the box off the rack.*

INT. FACTORY – DAY

         *SELMA daydreams, gazing across the machinery
         as she works. Her mind is far away. SELMA pulls
         herself together and wakes up. She notices that
         KATHY is monitoring her from her own machine.
         SELMA nods at her reassuringly.*

INT. FACTORY LOCKER ROOM – DAY

SELMA lugs two wooden boxes into the locker room. KATHY is getting changed. She looks up at her.

KATHY   Since when did you decide to do two at once?

SELMA   Thought I might as well. Don't worry, I'll card them.

KATHY shakes her head. NORMAN pokes his head in.

NORMAN   10 o'clock then, Selma.

SELMA nods awkwardly. NORMAN leaves.

KATHY   10 o'clock? What's this?

SELMA   Norman got me onto the night shift tonight.

KATHY   The night shift? You're crazy. You can hardly see well enough to work your own shift!

SELMA   I need the money, Kathy.

KATHY   If your father knew what you were going through for his sake – No, you can't do it, Selma. You've already done a full shift. I'm telling Norman it's downright irresponsible.

SELMA   You always take things so badly. If you don't take
         things badly you can do a whole load more than
         you think you can. Tonight suits me fine. It's just
         after drama club.

KATHY   And you're going to that, too! You're nuts. You
         shoulda dropped out weeks ago. I've sure had it
         up to my ears with that ridiculous show.

SELMA   But it gives me so much strength afterwards,
         Kathy. I've noticed that. I know it's only for fun,
         and that some of the others laugh at me, but in a
         way that show is what keeps everything together.

         *KATHY looks at her. Then she suddenly gets to
         her feet.*

KATHY   *(angrily)* No, I've had my fill of you, Selma.
         Do what you want. Do the night shift, go ahead,
         break your neck. Don't even for a second think
         I'm coming to your rescue!

         KATHY puts on her coat and stalks out.

EXT. FACTORY – EVENING

         *SELMA exits. The factory horn sounds.
         She carries her two boxes. She looks around.
         JEFF is waiting beside his pick-up.*

JEFF   Kathy split already.

SELMA   I know it. She wasn't who I was looking for.

JEFF   Oh? Who were you looking for?

SELMA   You. I was going to ask if you felt like giving me a
           ride. I'm without my bike today.

           JEFF looks suspicious.

SELMA   *(smiles)* Well, what do you say? A lift would be
           lovely. I am going to drama rehearsal. You mind?

JEFF   *(looks down)* That's why I'm here. I want to look
           after you, you know. Where's your bike, anyway?
           You always ride your bike.

           He takes the boxes.

SELMA   *(heading for his pick-up)* I figured it was
           quicker to walk.

JEFF   How'd you reckon that?

SELMA   I walked along the railroad tracks.

           JEFF glances up towards the railroad.
           He gets into the pick-up. There is a withered old
           bouquet inside.

JEFF   Maybe you want the flowers too? I guess I'll have to buy some new ones.

SELMA   *(smiles)* No, thanks. I don't want flowers and I don't want to be looked after. I just want a ride so I can rehearse my musical.

JEFF   *(starts the car)* You are crazy about musicals, Selma. Hey, why **do** they suddenly start to sing and dance? I mean, me, I don't suddenly start singing and dancing...

SELMA   *(smiles)* No, Jeff... you are right... you don't.

INT. REHEARSAL ROOMS – EVENING

A dozen PEOPLE are seated in the rehearsal room, SAMUEL and BORIS among them. The whole CAST is assembled. SAMUEL steps on stage with SELMA. JEFF sits down at the back of the room. He looks up at her.

SAMUEL We agree to get everyone together after you clock out and now you say Kathy isn't coming after all? Jeez, what a mess.

SELMA   She'll come next time. She's completely hooked.

SAMUEL Sure she is. We'll just have to make do.

Let's introduce you to the rest of the cast.
And your understudy, too.

SELMA   My understudy?

SAMUEL   Sure, you always have two in case one gets sick.
         A girl Boris knows. Suzan. She's a good dancer –
         but she doesn't have an ounce of your charisma.

         *SELMA looks at SUZAN, the gorgeous girl sitting
         next to BORIS. SAMUEL leads SUZAN and
         SELMA center stage.*

SAMUEL   Well, guys, here are our two Marias. You'll be
         seeing both of them at Sunday's rehearsal.
         As you can see, Selma wears glasses, but as
         Maria, she'll probably be best off without them.

         *SAMUEL looks at SELMA. She gets the idea she
         has to take off her glasses. She lets everyone see
         her without glasses. She blinks shyly. Then she
         puts them on again.*

SAMUEL   I'm really pleased with Selma's Maria. Without the
         glasses, it's perfect.

         *SELMA is still adjusting her eyes after putting her
         glasses back on.*

INT. FACTORY – NIGHT

A WOMAN shows SELMA what to do.

WOMAN   We are fewer at night, so you gotta get your own
material... and you also have to do your own
cutting. So you have to keep on workin' or else
there be nothing for Henry to do... that's why it's
better paid at night...

SELMA nods. She looks at HENRY at the next
machine.

SELMA   Is there less light than in the daytime?

WOMAN   It's exactly the same, you'll see.

She goes off, leaving SELMA on her own among
the noisy machines. SELMA does her very best.
But things soon start going wrong.

SELMA can't keep up when she has to cut the
sinks with the machine scissors, and it is hard for
her to see. Too often, HENRY has nothing to do.
The WOMAN looks at SELMA.

WOMAN   You have to feed Henry...

SELMA does her best. It goes better... but,
rushing to fetch the plates, she drops them on the
floor. As she picks them up, SELMA shakes her

head. HENRY is waiting, but she has nothing for
him. Suddenly he is handed material. SELMA
turns around... It's KATHY who has stepped in.

SELMA   Kathy! What are you doing here?

KATHY   What do you think? I've worked the night
         shift before. You have to run double fast.
         It takes a little while to get used to, when you
         must cut also.

         SELMA smiles at KATHY, who helps SELMA get
         the plates and cuts for her now and then. As they
         toil away, NORMAN comes by. He is putting on
         his coat, ready to go home.

NORMAN   Kathy? I didn't put you down for the night shift.

KATHY   Run along, Norman. I'm on my own time now.
         How I spend it is my business. And I want to
         spend it with Selma.

         NORMAN smiles and leaves.

NORMAN   Night night!

SELMA   Good night, Norman.

         She gives him a smile. Then she looks at KATHY,
         who smiles briefly.

INT. FACTORY – NIGHT

SELMA works the row on her own. KATHY perches on a chair, watching her. She glances down the second row.

KATHY   *(seriously)* Get more plates in one go… then you will make it…

SELMA   Yes, I know it, I'm on my way – go home, Kathy. You can go on home now. You got to get up in the morning. Thanks for helping me, though.

KATHY   *(looks at her without smiling)*
I'll just sit here and keep an eye out for you.

SELMA   You really don't have to. I can see perfectly well now. It's just sometimes, when I get very tired – it gets so dark. Honest, you can go home now, no worry.

KATHY   *(angrily)* Selma, I'm not going to argue with you.

SELMA   *(with a little smile)* Okay, stay then – please yourself – Cvalda!

SELMA thinks for a while.

SELMA   I like you better when you dance. You are happier when you dance. Why don't you dance a little?!

KATHY   Hey, concentrate on what you're doing. I'll dance
          when there is music. Now work.

          *KATHY glowers angrily at SELMA but doesn't say
          a word. SELMA concentrates.*

INT. FACTORY – NIGHT

          *SELMA works, busy, but tired. KATHY has
          dropped off to sleep in her chair. SELMA looks at
          her affectionately. A WORKER at the other end of
          the hall starts a machine. It emits another
          rhythmic beat into the hall. SELMA tries not to be
          distracted. But the music starts.*

INT. FACTORY – NIGHT

          Song: 'Cvalda'
          *SELMA starts up the music with great
          enthusiasm. Once it has started she wants KATHY
          to dance as she promised. But it takes time to get
          KATHY to become Cvalda. It is only after the
          'Stomp interlude' that KATHY is the smiling and
          dancing star that SELMA so much likes to see.*

SELMA   Clatter, crash, clack,
          Racket, bang, thump,
          Rattle, clang, crack,
          Thud, whack, bam...

THE WORKERS

  Clatter, crash, clack,
  Racket, bang, thump,

SELMA *(on top)* It's music
  Now dance!

THE WORKERS

  Rattle, clang, crack,
  Thud, whack, bam...

SELMA Darling Kathy, listen closely
  Cvalda's longing for a dance
  She deserves it, set her free...

THE WORKERS

  Clatter, crash and clack,
  Racket, bang and thump,
  Rattle, clang and crack,
  Thud, whack, bam!

SELMA Clatter-machines greet you and say
  We tap out a rhythm and sweep you away.
  A clatter-machine, what a magical sound,
  A room full of noises that spins you around...

  Stomp interlude

KATHY Darling Selma, look I'm dancing
  Faster than a shooting star,
  Cvalda's here, Cvalda sings...

THE WORKERS

> Clatter, crash and clack,
> Racket, bang and thump,
> Rattle, clang and crack,
> Thud, whack, bam...

KATHY/SELMA

> Clatter-machines greet us and say,
> We tap out a rhythm and sweep you away.
> A clatter-machine, what a magical sound,
> A room full of noises that spins us around...

SELMA is dancing around with the plates for the machine, but she forgets to take out a finished sink. We see this clearly. She puts in a new plate and starts the machine. This is also shown in the handle camera mode. Suddenly there is a loud noise.

INT. FACTORY – NIGHT

KATHY wakes up as the machine is cracking. Everybody runs to the machine. SELMA is desperately trying to stop the machine and get the plates out. She takes off her glove to get a better grip. She cuts her hands trying.

EXT. FACTORY – NIGHT

> *SELMA and KATHY step out into the streetlight's glare. SELMA shivers in the cold. KATHY peers around. JEFF waits in the pick-up.*

KATHY   *(to JEFF with feigned jocularity)* Do you live here? Did you know she was working tonight? If not, you sure got here early!

> *JEFF shrugs his shoulders.*

JEFF   Sure, I knew. When it's this late she might say yes to a ride, who knows!

> *SELMA smiles.*

SELMA   It'd be better if you took Kathy home; she has to get up in a few hours…

> *JEFF looks at her bloody hand.*

JEFF   You cut your hand—

SELMA   Yes, those plates are sharp.

> *SELMA hugs KATHY.*

SELMA   I'll walk. I could do with a bit of fresh air—

> *SELMA smiles and makes her way up the slope to*

> the railroad tracks. She turns and smiles to
> KATHY.

SELMA   Thanks for helping me, Kathy.

> KATHY waves. JEFF gets in, starts the engine.
> KATHY watches SELMA, who makes her way
> along the track. She can't stay on course for long
> without discreetly finding the rail with her foot,
> and using it to guide her. KATHY notices and
> understands SELMA's little ploy. KATHY is
> profoundly affected. She weeps a little. JEFF
> reaches over and opens the pick-up door for her.
> She wipes her eyes and smiles to him.

KATHY   It's nothing. Thanks, I sure appreciate the ride.

> KATHY gets in. They set off.

EXT. RAILROAD TRACK BEHIND BILL AND LINDA'S HOUSE – NIGHT

> SELMA walks down the tracks all alone.
> She advances purposefully in the early morning
> light. She walks onto a bridge. She senses this,
> and turns around. She walks back a bit, and
> fumbles her way down the embankment,
> through the fence, and into the garden where
> her trailer stands.

EXT. BILL AND LINDA'S HOUSE – NIGHT

> SELMA knocks at the door gently. BILL answers
> it. He puts a finger to his lips, then goes back
> inside for GENE, who is asleep. BILL carries him
> carefully towards the trailer.

SELMA   *(whispers)* Thank you for looking after Mr. G.

BILL   No problem. Jeff drove your hairpins over in his
pick-up; I left them on the table.

SELMA   Thanks so much.

> They go quietly into the trailer.

INT. TRAILER – NIGHT

> Gently, BILL puts GENE into bed. SELMA loosens
> Gene's clothes and puts a blanket over him. They
> close the door quietly behind them. They go into
> the living area. SELMA sits down wearily at the
> table. She pushes the two boxes to one side,
> rests her head on the table. She closes her eyes
> for a moment.

SELMA   My eyes are crazy tonight.

> BILL stands there self-consciously.

BILL   I think I've found a solution to my problem,
            Selma.

SELMA   *(brightens)* Oh, Bill, how happy that makes me!

BILL   Hey, it's nothing special. But I've made up my
            mind. I'm going to tell Linda. After all, she loves
            me. We'll grapple with this thing together.

SELMA   *(nods)* That's a good idea. It really is.

BILL   I mean, it's only money.

            SELMA sits there a moment, smiling.
            She is almost nodding off. BILL notices.

BILL   I'm sorry, I'll let you get to bed.

SELMA   Yes, I guess I'm a bit tired.

            BILL goes to the door.
            Then he turns and looks at SELMA.

BILL   Good night, Selma.

SELMA   *(rubbing her eyes)* Good night, Bill. And
            thank you.

            BILL opens the door. But he does not leave.
            He looks at SELMA. Then he closes the door with
            a bang. He withdraws into the semi-darkness

behind the door. SELMA sits for a while, and
then gets up, goes to the door, and locks it.
BILL holds his breath. She is very close to him
now, but she doesn't see him. She sits down at
the table again. She fumbles in her bag and pulls
out some dollar bills clipped to the receipt she
got for the hairpins. She removes the receipt and
folds the bills. Then she crosses to the loose
panel and extracts the tin. She puts the money
into it. She looks around as if she senses
somebody's presence, but calms down again,
and replaces the tin behind the panel. BILL holds
his breath in the corner.

INT. CINEMA – EVENING

KATHY and SELMA watch Top Hat again.
Fred has just sung 'Cheek to cheek' and he is
dancing with Ginger. KATHY mostly looks sadly at
SELMA. SELMA mostly listens.

SELMA   What now?

KATHY   (looks briefly at the screen) He's leading.

The ANGRY MAN from last time is sitting behind
them again.

ANGRY MAN
Shhhh!

KATHY   (leans close to SELMA and whispers) Side by side.

               KATHY takes SELMA's hand. With two fingers she
               does the dance on SELMA's palm, imitating the
               steps she sees on the screen. It is easy to see
               that she is doing the same characteristic cross-
               overs that Fred and Ginger are doing. SELMA
               giggles, impressed. KATHY weeps as her fingers
               dance on.

EXT. CINEMA – EVENING

               KATHY and SELMA emerge from the cinema.
               KATHY holds SELMA by the hand. SELMA stops.

SELMA   I know you don't like it, but I am going to drama
               now. You think I should drop it, but my eyes are
               actually better lately.

KATHY   (looks at her tenderly) I don't think anything –
               Listen, we'll both go.

SELMA   (happily surprised) I thought you'd had enough?

KATHY   I'll give it one last chance.

               KATHY leads SELMA away. SELMA squeezes
               her hand.

SELMA   I can play that part. I know I can. My heart says so... *(she smiles)* Anyway it says that it would have been a pity to learn all the words otherwise...

INT. REHEARSAL ROOM – NIGHT

SELMA stands without her glasses, next to KATHY, who waits just off-stage. BORIS is at the front of the stage. The SEVEN KIDS playing his children stand in the background. The song leads up to SELMA's entrance.

SEVEN KIDS
'So long, farewell, auf wiedersehn, good night,'

BOY   'I hate to go and leave this pretty sight.'

SAMUEL —And!

SELMA is rooted to the spot. KATHY looks at her. SELMA clutches KATHY's hand.

KATHY   You're on.

SELMA   *(whispers hesitantly)* It really is darker tonight.
        (dons glasses, peers through them briefly)
        I can't even see him. I hope there'll be more light
        when we do the actual show—

KATHY   He's at the front of the stage. On the other side.

SELMA   How far would you say it was?

KATHY shakes her head quietly and looks sympathetically at SELMA. BORIS looks at them in confusion.

SAMUEL   *(from the auditorium)* Enter Selma! Again, please.

The piano tries again.

SEVEN KIDS

'So long, farewell, auf wiedersehn, good night,'

BOY   'I hate to go and leave this pretty sight.'

Some time passes. KATHY appears on stage, crosses the gap from the wings to BORIS in measured steps.

SAMUEL   No, no – Selma comes on now! Can't you hear?

KATHY   *(smiles apologetically)* Oh, sorry!

KATHY exits, returning to SELMA.
SAMUEL sighs.

SAMUEL   Try again!

KATHY   *(whispers)* Four big steps and one little one. And you'll be there.

SELMA nods.

SEVEN KIDS
    'So long, farewell, auf wiedersehn, good night,'

BOY   'I hate to go and leave this pretty sight.'

KATHY guides SELMA in the right direction with a gentle push. SELMA walks slowly towards BORIS. KATHY hardly dares to watch. SELMA takes six big steps and one little one. She ends up more or less in the right spot.

SAMUEL   That was good. Perfect timing. Now you do your lines. You could dance in a circle around him while you sing. Or maybe you have a better idea to suggest?

SELMA stands motionless, peering into the auditorium. A long silence. She doesn't move.

SAMUEL   Or maybe you don't want to suggest anything?

SELMA takes a deep breath.

SELMA   Samuel, I want to talk to you. Outside.

SAMUEL   *(surprised)* Sure, Selma, but if it's about the drums, let me tell you, I've been looking everywhere – you'll get your drums, don't worry!

SELMA   It's not that—

SAMUEL   No? All right, hey, of course we can go outside
         for a chat – of course we can—
         (to BORIS as he exits)
         Rehearse a bit with Suzan while I'm gone.

         KATHY appears. She takes SELMA by the arm.
         SUZAN gets ready.

INT. CORRIDOR – NIGHT

         SELMA waits for SAMUEL. He walks up to her.

SAMUEL   Okay, Selma. What's wrong?

SELMA   I am thinking maybe I shouldn't play Maria, after
         all. I'm much too old – and maybe it doesn't
         matter so much to me after all – the show I mean
         – matter enough for me to take it seriously
         enough. After all, it's a lot of work.

SAMUEL   It sure is—

SELMA   And Suzan is such a good dancer, I think – much
         better than me – isn't there another part I could
         play? A smaller part?

SAMUEL   *(scrutinizes her)* Everyone's been cast. Well, apart
         from the old nun who lets Maria out of the

convent gate – you can have her part, but she doesn't do any dancing.

SELMA   *(disappointed)* Oh…

SAMUEL   *(registering her disappointment)*
          But maybe she could.

SELMA   (smiles freshly) Taps?

SAMUEL   I told you there is no tapping in *Sound of Music*.

          He looks at her a little while. Then he softens up.

SAMUEL   Okay, Selma… you can do a shuffle. But very small, Selma. Almost as if it wasn't taps…

          He shows her some very, very soft steps.

SELMA   *(smiles)* Okay, Samuel! I'd like that. I'd be in the show after all.

SAMUEL   *(smiles and nods)* And it'd make sense for the nun to wear glasses, with her being so old and all.

          SELMA smiles at him.

SELMA   Thank you, Samuel. You're not angry with me, are you?

SAMUEL   Of course not, Selma.

> *SAMUEL looks across at the other members of the cast.*

SAMUEL   But it means you won't be on tonight. We're not doing the convent today.

SELMA   That's fine. I'll just watch for a bit.
         (takes SAMUEL by the arm, earnestly)
         Thank you, Samuel – thank you for letting me stay in the show. It means an awful lot to me.

SAMUEL   Sure, Selma. Few people deserve to be included as much as you do—

INT. REHEARSAL ROOM – NIGHT

> *SELMA and KATHY sit in the auditorium, watching the others rehearse. SAMUEL, closer to the front, talks to some of the CAST MEMBERS. They glance over at SELMA. On stage, SUZAN and BORIS dance. SELMA smiles at the sound. KATHY looks at her with mercy. Then she gives her a little squeeze.*

INT. FACTORY – DAY

> *SELMA tends her machine; KATHY glances at*

her. She waves. SELMA sees her wave, smiles, and waves back. SELMA is working well. She is concentrating hard. NORMAN enters. He looks at SELMA. Then he comes up to her.

NORMAN *(cheerfully)* Where are all the hairpins today? I'm ashamed of myself, going on my break and not poking pins into cards for old Oldrich!

SELMA They're at home. I only card them at home in the evenings now. So I don't get everything mixed up. The folks back home will just have to wait a bit longer for their money. If you do too much at once you end up doing it all badly. And so I won't be working nights any more, either.

KATHY And she's dropped Maria, too.

NORMAN *(with uncertain joviality)* Well, well, well. What you reckon I'm gonna do if I can't bawl you out for learning your lines on company time?

SELMA smiles as she works. NORMAN fidgets. He can't get himself to leave. KATHY looks at him, worried. He gives her a look.

SELMA *(cheerfully)* Hey, shoo now. Let us get some work done!

NORMAN pulls himself together.

NORMAN *(seriously)* I want a word, Selma, alright?
In my office.

SELMA looks up.

SELMA   Can it wait 'till lunch?

NORMAN No, 'fraid not.

INT. FACTORY SUPERVISOR'S OFFICE – DAY

SELMA is seated. She peers around the office.
NORMAN sits at his desk.

NORMAN *(suffering)* I hate saying this, but we were down
for a day when the machine broke...

SELMA   I can do my job just fine as long as I stick to the
day shift, and keep my mind on it. I promise I can
– it won't happen again.

NORMAN begins to protest. SELMA cuts him off.

SELMA   I promise, Norman. I mean, I know you're the one
who gets the blame. I just have to quit dreaming
so much – I forgot, but from now on I'll
remember—

NORMAN *(shakes his head)* I've been ordered to let you
go, Selma—

SELMA   Let me go?

NORMAN It's not your first mistake, we all know that.
        They won't take any more chances – It's out of
        my hands.

SELMA   *(frowns and thinks)* You mean I have to just – get
        up and go?

NORMAN *(intensely miserable)* Yes, Selma. But you won't
        have to pay for the damaged machine, I did get
        them to agree to that—

        *NORMAN pushes an envelope with SELMA's
        wages across the desk. SELMA is shaken. She
        looks into the hall. SELMA looks at NORMAN.*

SELMA   *(quietly)* Thanks, Norman.

NORMAN I don't know what to say—

SELMA   You don't have to say anything – you've always
        been kind to me. You are a good man to work for.
        I like you very much.

        *NORMAN looks at her and shakes his head.
        SELMA gets up and picks up the envelope.*

SELMA   Goodbye, Norman.

NORMAN Goodbye, Selma.

SELMA turns and opens the door into the factory.

NORMAN   Maybe I could find you something away from the
         machines where your eyesight wouldn't matter so
         much – not right away, but—

SELMA   *(on her way out)* Sure – thank you, Norman.

INT. FACTORY – DAY

         *SELMA, changed into her day clothes, walks
         through the factory towards the exit. Several
         WORKERS watch her go. She smiles at them.
         They acknowledge her smiles. SELMA stops next
         to a row of machines by the window.*

SELMA   *(asking into space)* Is Morty at his machine?

         MORTY appears from farther down the row.

MORTY   Right here, Selma.

         He comes up to her. He is grave.

SELMA   I have two boxes back home. But I'm not finished
         with them. Can I return them and still get my
         deposit back?

MORTY   We'll figure something out, Selma. Sure we will.

SELMA   Because I've got to scrape together all I can, and
         just hope it'll be enough.

         She nods to herself and heads for the exit.
         NORMAN is talking to KATHY. KATHY angers.
         She runs after SELMA.

KATHY   They can't do this! You've never done any
         damage 'till now. They got no right! If you go,
         I go.

         KATHY turns to NORMAN, who has come
         after her.

KATHY   I'm going, too, Norman. I'm sure you can find a
         whole new crew of folks who can mind your
         goddamned machines for you.

         SELMA turns to KATHY.

SELMA   Don't argue, please don't. You're always
         yelling at each other. It doesn't sound nice
         and it's time somebody told you. Excuse me,
         but I've got to go.

         KATHY looks at SELMA. She is distraught.

KATHY   How will you get by?
         (looks at NORMAN furiously)
         What is she going to do now? Did you even
         bother to think of that?

SELMA   No need to worry about me. If there ever is,
         I'll let you know.

         SELMA gives KATHY a hug.

SELMA   See you around!

         SELMA nods to NORMAN again and goes out.
         KATHY watches her go.

EXT. FACTORY PARKING LOT – DAY

         SELMA emerges out onto the parking lot.
         She looks around. SOMEONE is watching from
         a doorway.

SELMA   Has anyone seen Jeff today?

PERSON IN DOORWAY
         He usually gets here early, Selma; but not
         this early.

SELMA   *(snorts)* If he'd been here today, I'd have let him
         drive me home.

         She follows the fence to the embankment and
         sets off along the railroad tracks.

SELMA   *(to herself)* I could have done with a ride today.

EXT. RAILROAD TRACKS – DAY

> SELMA walks along the tracks, her foot against the rail. JEFF appears far behind her, running hard. He catches up, out of breath.

JEFF   I just spotted you! I can give you a lift if you like...

SELMA   *(smiles)* That's nice. Later on. Can you come by later on? I could use a 'lift' then.

JEFF   Right.

> He walks on with her. She stops and turns towards him. She smiles.

SELMA   Not now!

JEFF   No, sure – I was just—

SELMA   *(smiles)* And you'll need your truck if you're going to give me a lift, won't you?

> JEFF nods.

SELMA   Come by my place about threeish. I've got something I need to do then.

> JEFF nods and leaves reluctantly. SELMA stands there and listens. There is utter silence. She looks up again to see where JEFF is.

SELMA   (shouts) Get off the track, Jeff! There is a train!

JEFF stands there a moment; he can't hear a thing.
Then in the distance a timber train can be heard.
He steps aside. SELMA goes a little way down the
embankment, too. The train passes. It is endless.
Nothing but cars laden with timber. It moves
infinitely slowly. On top of a couple of the cars 20
WORKERS are perched, taking a ride on their way
to a new job. They look down at JEFF and SELMA.

As the train passes by, JEFF notices that SELMA
seems to be in doubt as to where to look for him,
as she can't hear him in the noise. He throws a
little rock that lands close to her. She looks in that
direction and speaks.

SELMA   (with a smile) Off you go then!

JEFF   You don't see, do you?

SELMA turns toward his voice, surprised to hear
where he really is. She's unhappy to have been
fooled by his trick.

SELMA   What is there to see?

SELMA stands motionless as the train rumbles by.
Now she hears the rhythm of the wheels as they
cross a gap in the rails. The slow beat persists,
and she smiles.

EXT. RAILROAD TRACKS – DAY

> Song: 'I have seen it all'

> SELMA hears the music that comes in the
> noise from the train. She dances along – the train
> is her faith and she follows. She is trying to
> convince herself that turning blind is not so bad.
> JEFF wants to make her admit that there is still
> so much to see. But when he asks the worst
> questions they make SELMA freeze for a minute
> in pain. Around her in the field and by the house
> PEOPLE illustrate her longing for the safe
> domestic life. But on the train the WORKERS
> dance and support her. In the end they take her
> with them as JEFF is being left behind on the
> trail. They carry her high in the air.

SELMA   I've seen it all, I've seen the willow-trees,
            I've seen my land on the first day of peace,
            I've seen a friend killed by a friend,
            And lives that were over before they were spent.
            I've seen what I was – I know what I'll be
            I've seen it all – there is no more to see!

JEFF   You haven't seen elephants, kings or Peru!

SELMA   I'm happy to say I had better to do…

JEFF   What about China? You've seen the Great Wall?

SELMA   All walls are great, if the roof doesn't fall...

JEFF   And the man you will marry?
        The home you will share?

SELMA   Oh, no, but I really, I really don't care...

JEFF   You've never been to the Niagara Falls?

SELMA   I have seen water, it's water, that's all...

JEFF   The Eiffel Tower, the Empire State?

SELMA   My pulse was as high on my very first date.

JEFF   Your grandson's hands as he plays with
        your hair?

SELMA   Oh, no, I really, I really don't c—
        I've seen it all, I've seen the dark
        I've seen the brightness in one little spark.
        I've seen what I chose – and I've seen what I need,
        And that is enough. To want more would be greed.
        I've seen what I was – and I know what I'll be
        I've seen it all – there is no more to see!

ALL (NOT SELMA AND JEFF)
        You've seen it all and all you have seen
        Is there to review on your own little screen
        The light and the dark, the big and the small
        Just keep in mind – you need no more at all

You've seen what you were – and know what
you'll be
You've seen it all – you don't need to see!

*As the music is about to end in the musical
scene, the train disappears in the distance.*

EXT. RAILROAD TRACKS – DAY

*But, back in reality when the song stops, the train
is still thundering by, as close to SELMA and
JEFF as it was when the song began.*

JEFF   You don't see, do you?

SELMA   I had the sun in my eyes. Please, dear Jeff, go
            now... and come back with your car at three!

*JEFF looks at her a while. SELMA looks calmly at
him. He stands another moment. She looks at him
pleadingly. He turns around and walks a little.
Turns again... But she still looks at him. He turns
and leaves.*

INT./EXT. TRAILER – DAY

*SELMA enters the empty trailer. She takes the
envelope with her wages out of her shoulder bag.
She quickly retrieves the taffy tin from behind the*

panel. She puts it onto the table and opens it.
She fumbles inside. It is empty. She fumbles
again. She stops, motionless. She puts the
envelope back into her bag and goes outside.

EXT./INT. BILL AND LINDA'S HOUSE – DAY

       SELMA knocks. The wind is blowing.
       LINDA answers the door.

LINDA   *(discomforted by SELMA's arrival)* Hello, Selma.
       You're early today. Gene hasn't come back yet.

SELMA   I just wanted a word with Bill.

       LINDA nods and looks down.

LINDA   He took the day off to go to the bank for his box.

       LINDA looks up at SELMA.

LINDA   I know everything, Selma. Bill told me! I want you
       to move out.

SELMA   What do you know, Linda?

LINDA   That you came onto him and asked him up to the
       trailer – but he turned you down.

       SELMA looks at her for a moment. Then she nods.

LINDA   *(angrily)* You got nothing to say for yourself?

SELMA   *(calmly, shrugging her shoulders)* No. May I talk
         to Bill, Linda? Please!

INT./EXT. BILL AND LINDA'S HOUSE – DAY

SELMA walks gravely through the house.
LINDA is sitting at the table in the living room.
She eats a biscuit in silence. Now she crumbles
the last bit of it in her hand and lets the crumbs
fall down on the table. She opens the door into
the study at the back of the house. She enters,
closing door quietly behind her. BILL, in semi-
darkness, sits at his desk, not in uniform, his face
buried in his hands. In front of him is a bag from
the local Savings and Loan. Bundles of dollar bills
poke out, and beside it is the deposit box from
the bank. The turntable is in the study now; he
has put on an easy-listening record.

SELMA   Hello, Bill.

BILL   *(looks up, red-eyed)* Hello, Selma.

SELMA   You couldn't tell her, after all?

BILL   *(shakes his head)* No. I tried to shoot myself, but I
         couldn't do that either.

SELMA   Poor you.

BILL   Linda saw me up at the trailer. I told her it
         was you who wanted... that you'd fallen in love
         with me.

SELMA   Yes, Linda told me.

BILL   And what did you tell her?

SELMA   Nothing.

BILL   You didn't tell her I was lying? Why not?

SELMA   *(calmly)* We promised we'd keep each other's
         secrets. Mum's the word, right?

         BILL looks at her and shakes his head.
         SELMA screws up her eyes.

SELMA   My eyes are pretty bad today. But isn't that a lot
         of money you've got there?

         BILL looks at the bag from the Savings and Loan.
         Then he tucks the exposed bills back into it.

BILL   It's a bag from the bank.

SELMA   *(nods)* Linda said you went to get the box. You
         put the money in that bag as if it'd been in the
         vaults, right?

BILL   I went to the bank to ask for more time. But then
            I couldn't do it. So I went down to the vault and
            brought the box home instead. I've done that a
            couple of times recently, even though it's been
            empty. Linda always gets so proud when I sit in
            here with it. *(he smiles faintly)* But yesterday she
            asked to see the money…

SELMA   But it is my money, Bill. You know that, and I
            have to have the money back.

BILL   *(slightly confused)* Yes, of course.

            *BILL pulls the bills out of the bag and looks at
            them. He puts them back.*

BILL   *(nods)* You can have it back in a month. One
            month and I'll pay you back. I just have to meet
            this month's installment. I only need to borrow it
            for one month.

            SELMA stands there silently.

SELMA   No, Bill. It's no good. I need it now. I want to pay
            the doctor this afternoon. I won't be able to save
            up any more. That's over now. I want to pay what
            I've got – while I've still got it.

BILL   Selma, a month. That's all I'm asking. Show a
            little kindness! Gene doesn't turn 13 until after
            Christmas!

SELMA   *(shakes her head)* No, Bill. I need my money now,
          if you don't mind—

          BILL gazes at her stiffly. He doesn't move. SELMA
          puts out her hand. She fumbles her way to the
          bag in his hand. She takes it.

SELMA   There was $2026 and ten cents in the tin. I can't
          count it, but I trust you. Plus my money from
          work today—

          She gets her wages out of her shoulder-bag.
          She puts the money into the bank bag.

SELMA   That makes $2056 and 10 cents. It'll be enough –
          it has to be.

          She puts the bank bag into her shoulder bag.
          She turns to go. BILL suddenly gets to his feet.
          He quickly unlocks his desk drawer and pulls out
          his revolver. He points it at SELMA.

BILL   Stop, Selma.

          SELMA shows no sign of stopping.

BILL   I'm pointing my gun at you, Selma.

          SELMA turns around, smiling.

SELMA   I don't believe you, Bill. I can't see a gun. I think
        you're just trying to fool me.

BILL   A month, Selma. Just a month.

SELMA   No, Bill.

        *SELMA turns to go. BILL stands there, gun in
        hand. Then he runs after her. He jabs the gun into
        her stomach.*

BILL   *(whispers)* Now do you believe I've got my gun?

        SELMA feels the gun.

SELMA   Yes, I believe you, Bill. But it is my money.

BILL   No, it's the money I had in my box, and you came
        here to steal it. STOP THIEF!

        BILL shouts.

BILL   Linda, LINDA!

        LINDA runs in.

LINDA   What's the matter, Bill?

        LINDA sees the gun pointing at SELMA.

BILL   *(frantically)* She's stealing our money, Linda! She

knew I had the gun in my drawer. She got her
hands on it and forced me to hand over the cash.
But I got my gun back.

LINDA looks at SELMA in horror.

LINDA   What are you doing, Selma? Why are you doing
         this? Is that why you wanted him – for his
         money?

         SELMA doesn't reply. She shakes her head.

BILL   Hurry, Linda. Get my handcuffs from the car. I'll
         arrest her.

         *LINDA looks around in confusion. Then she runs
         out. BILL keeps his gun in SELMA's tummy. Her
         hands are clasped around it, too.*

BILL   Give me the money and I'll let you go.

SELMA   Where would I go?

BILL   Give me the money. Gene doesn't even know
         you've got it.

         *He fumbles in her shoulder bag and takes the bag
         of money out. Suddenly SELMA is desperate.*

SELMA   *(screams)* No!

She twists around and tugs on the shoulder bag. He tries to grab her. The gun goes off. BILL collapses, the money bag in his hand. He has been hit in the shoulder. His other hand clutches his wounded shoulder. SELMA now holds the gun. From the police car, LINDA hears the shot.

BILL You shot me, Selma. I shoulda done it myself. I won't be able to live with this. It's a good thing you shot me.

SELMA kneels and reaches for the bag, but BILL grips it tightly. They wrestle for a moment but he won't let go. She points the gun at him.

SELMA Give it to me or I'll fire.

BILL *(shakes his head, whispers)* You'll have to kill me first, Selma. Kill me, Selma. It's what I deserve. I'm begging you—

LINDA runs in with the handcuffs. She stops in shock when she sees BILL lying on the floor, bleeding. SELMA has the gun trained on him.

BILL *(doesn't see LINDA; whispers, in tears)* Selma – I beg you! Show some mercy! I always treated you decent! Selma, I beg you!

BILL spots LINDA in the doorway. He looks at her for a moment.

BILL looks up at SELMA.

BILL   Run, Linda! She's got my gun!

        *SELMA turns towards LINDA, gun in hand; the
        gun happens to point at LINDA.*

BILL   Run! Run up to Miller's farm and alert the
        precinct. Tell them to hurry.

        *LINDA looks at him, and runs off. SELMA turns
        and points the gun at BILL. He looks up at her.*

BILL   You won't get the money until you've shot me!

        *She pulls at the bag but cannot get it away from
        him. She tilts her head, listens to the sound of the
        bit of wood on GENE's bike wheel. GENE is riding
        around the house. It is very noisy. SELMA aims
        the gun at BILL's arm.*

SELMA   I will shoot you in the arm, Bill.

        *She fires. But BILL has managed to turn the
        gun away from his arm towards his body.
        She hits him in the belly. GENE doesn't hear the
        shot over the noise of his bike. BILL still clutches
        the money. SELMA fires repeatedly. She hits him
        with the gun, but he won't let go. The gun is
        empty now.*

BILL   *(groans)* You gotta kill me first. Oh, Selma, kill me.
Do it for real. Please—

*Frantic, SELMA grabs the metal safe deposit
box, hits BILL with it repeatedly. Finally he is
motionless. She tears the blood-spattered money
bag from his fingers. She sits down, exhausted.
There's blood on the blouse she wears over her
dress. In the silence she notices the turntable.
The record finished ages ago, but the needle is
still clicking against the innermost groove. It utters
a fractured rhythm. SELMA goes into a dream.*

INT./EXT. BILL AND LINDA'S HOUSE AND EXT. BY THE RIVER – DAY

Song: 'Smith and Wesson'

*During the dance BILL gets up and cleans himself
up in the bathroom. He goes on making up the
house as if nothing has happened. He cleans up
the crumbs we saw LINDA drop on the table in
the living room. SELMA is confused and
miserable, and the BILL in the song comforts her
by acting as if there had never been a killing in
the house. When he hears the sirens from the
approaching police cars he helps SELMA on her
way to escape. In the garden she is met by
LINDA, who also tries to help. It is difficult for
SELMA to run, even though everybody tries to*

help her. GENE is going around on his bike,
making a noise, supporting his mother.

SELMA   Black night is falling,
The sun is gone to bed.
The innocent are dreaming.
As you should sleepyhead.
Sleepyhead, sleepyhead.

SELMA   Does it hurt?

BILL   I hurt you much more
So don't you worry!

SELMA   I don't know what to do.
Everything just feels so wrong.

BILL   Everything is fine.
Just stay strong.

SELMA   Silly Selma, you're the one to blame.

GENE   You just did what you had to do.
You just did what you had to do.
You just did what you had to do.
You just did what you had to do.

SELMA   The time it takes a tear to fall
A snake to shed its skin
Is all the time that's needed to forgive
Forgive me!

BILL   You are forgiven
            (he hears a distant siren)
            Come on hurry!

            *BREAK in the music as the gramophone cannot
            be heard anymore. SELMA stands for a little while
            in silence until she is again attracted by a sound
            that can carry the music along – the sound of the
            flag line in the wind, slapping against the flagpole.
            This break is also filmed with handle camera.*

SELMA   I killed your man.

LINDA   I did it myself. Hurry! I called the police.
            They are just down the road.

SELMA   They've come for me,
            Why should I run?

LINDA   They'll take your money!
            Run for your boy.

SELMA   Silly Selma, you're the one to blame.

GENE   You just did what you had to do.
            You just did what you had to do.
            You just did what you had to do.
            You just did what you had to do.

SELMA   The time it takes a tear to fall
            A heart to miss a beat

A snake to shed its skin
A rose to grow a thorn
Is all the time that's needed
To forgive me.
I am so sorry.
I just did what I had to do.
I just did what I had to do.
I just did what I had to do.
I just did what I had to do.

SELMA is dancing more and more crazily in the water where the river is deepest. The sirens from the police cars are getting close now. Just as SELMA is about to disappear into the water a hand grabs her.

EXT. BY THE RIVER – DAY

JEFF has seized SELMA, who was close to the edge of the water. He grabs her before she falls in.

JEFF   Selma! You shouldn't go so close to the water... not when your eyes are so poor...

SELMA   Jeff! What are you doing here?

JEFF   We had a date – I was going to give you a lift – I saw you from the bridge.

SELMA   *(puzzled)* Is it already threeish?

JEFF   *(ashamed)* Not quite – but hell, I'm always early. If
         now is not the right time I can come back later—

         *SELMA thinks. She hears the sirens in the
         distance. Then she smiles at him.*

SELMA   Now's probably the best time, after all.

         *SELMA takes him by the hand. He's surprised.
         She leads him to his pick-up. JEFF notices the
         blood on SELMA's hands and blouse.*

JEFF   Look, you've cut yourself again – it's all over your
         blouse—

         They get in. JEFF looks up at SELMA.

JEFF   Where to?

SELMA   The highway – it'll be a long ride—

JEFF   Where are you going?

SELMA   You gonna drive me or not?

         *JEFF starts the pick-up. They turn right down the
         bigger road. Two police cars appear from the
         other direction and turn towards the house.
         JEFF sees them in his mirror.*

JEFF   This place is crazy with cops—

SELMA   *(nods)* Yes, crazy—

INT. JEFF'S PICK-UP – DAY

> *SELMA sleeps, the shoulder bag on her lap.*
> *JEFF drapes his jacket around her shoulders as*
> *he drives along the empty roads through the*
> *forest. She looks like a perfectly satisfied child as*
> *she sleeps peacefully.*

INT. JEFF'S PICK-UP – EVENING

> *JEFF stops near a bus stop on the edge of town.*
> *To the right of the road is a field, with a path*
> *leading across it to a stand of trees. JEFF turns*
> *off the engine. He wakes up SELMA, putting a*
> *hand on her shoulder.*

JEFF   Selma—

SELMA   *(collecting herself)* Yes?

JEFF   We're here.

> *SELMA blinks into the semi-darkness.*

SELMA   The bus stop?

JEFF   Yes, it's right over there.

SELMA   *(nods)* Then we must be right next to the path.

            JEFF looks at her. SELMA straightens her hair and
            opens the door. She turns to the field.

JEFF   May I come with you?

SELMA   No, you may NOT come with me – this is my
            secret – I told you that!

            SELMA gets out. She walks warily to the path
            across the field. JEFF looks at her, concerned.

JEFF   May I wait for you, then?

SELMA   *(pauses briefly and considers)*
            Yes, wait for me. No harm can come of that.

            SELMA finds her way onto the little path.
            JEFF watches her go.

EXT. FOREST – EVENING

            SELMA follows the path into the forest. She looks
            up into the bright sky among the dark trees. In a
            clearing she halts, and feels her way along the
            right-hand side of the path. She proceeds with her
            hand stretched out ahead of her until she feels a

bench. She moves to the front of the bench and kneels down, facing away from it. In the direction the bench faces, she can feel the edge of a little lake. She takes the bloody money bag from her shoulder bag. She pulls out the money and puts it carefully into her shoulder bag. Then she takes off her bloody blouse. She bundles up the blouse and bag and throws them into the water. The blouse splashes as it hits the surface, and sinks, but the money bag gets stuck in some reeds. She doesn't notice. She gets to her feet and sets off.

EXT. FOREST – EVENING

SELMA reaches a point where several paths branch off. There is a sign. But it is blank. SELMA finds it. She runs her fingers over it. She feels a raised arrow on the wood of the sign. The arrow points down one of the paths. She sets off in that direction.

EXT. EDGE OF WOODS – EVENING

SELMA walks down the path, which narrows. She fumbles forward. She walks into a rope stretched between the trees. She takes it. She smiles. It leads to a group of large buildings with lights shining in their windows. The rope ends at a gate. SELMA rings a bell.

EXT./INT. HOSPITAL – EVENING

> An ORDERLY leads SELMA through hospital
> grounds. He leads her to a door on a corridor.
> He knocks for her. DR. POKORNÝ appears in
> casual attire and answers the door. He looks at
> the ORDERLY and nods. He takes SELMA's arm
> now and leads her inside, shutting the door
> behind him.

INT. DR. POKORNÝ'S OFFICE – EVENING

> SELMA sits on a chair. DR. POKORNÝ sits down
> too. He looks at her.

SELMA   *(in Czech)* Dobrý vecer, pane doktore!

DR. POKORNÝ
    (smiles lightly) Dobrý vecer!
    (switches to English)
    You've gotten worse, I see.

SELMA   It's about Evzên. I want you to operate on him.

DR. POKORNÝ
    I will have to examine him first.

SELMA   He has been examined back home. He is like me.
    I know you can give him operation and make his
    eyes good. That's what the doctor said in

Czechoslovakia – he admired you very much.
He said if anyone could do it, you could!

DR. POKORNÝ
> *(sits there quietly for a moment)*
> I can't make any promises.

SELMA　I know you can cure him.
> *(she reaches into her sling bag)*
> I have the money here. I'll send him to you –
> I know when it is time.

> *She puts all the money, coins included,*
> *onto the table.*

SELMA　There's $2056 and 10 cents here. It's not quite
what it costs, but it's all I could get together.
You think you can do it for that?

DR. POKORNÝ
> If I can do the operation, I can do it for that.

SELMA　*(smiles)* This is wonderful! So we have a deal.

> *DR. POKORNÝ looks at the money. He gets*
> *up and crosses to his desk. He gets out a pad*
> *of forms.*

DR. POKORNÝ
> What name shall I put on the receipt?
> What did you say your name was?

SELMA   Oh, I don't need a receipt. No, really I don't.

DR. POKORNÝ

But I have to know your son's name – for when
he comes in for his operation.

SELMA ponders.

DR. POKORNÝ

Evzên... and his last name?

SELMA   *(in doubt; then an idea occurs)* Nový! If you ask
him he will tell you his last name is Nový, and
then you'll know he's been paid for.

DR. POKORNÝ

Nový? Like Oldrich Nový? The tap dancer? I saw
his films when I was a kid. He was in the first
musical I ever saw.

SELMA   *(smiles)* Same here.

DR. POKORNÝ

He was good back home but he never really
made it over here, did he?

*SELMA is lost in thought. Now she looks up. She
looks perplexed. DR. POKORNÝ looks up at her.*

DR. POKORNÝ

Yes?

SELMA   I just wondered how long you keep the
           bandage on. Not too long, I hope. I would hate
           him to be scared.

DR. POKORNÝ
           Don't worry, we only do one eye at a time.

SELMA   *(smiles in relief)* That's good. Now I must go.

           She gets up. DR. POKORNÝ looks at her.

DR. POKORNÝ
           You ought to start using a cane now.

SELMA   Thanks for the advice – but I'm afraid it won't be
           necessary.

**EXT./INT. JEFF'S PICK-UP BY THE ROADSIDE –
NIGHT**

           *JEFF sits in his car, in the dark. He hears
           something. It is SELMA. She opens the door and
           gets in. He looks at her.*

JEFF   I was afraid you couldn't find the pick-up in the
           dark.

SELMA   *(nods)* —but I did.

JEFF   Should I take you home?

SELMA   Yes, I suppose you should.

JEFF   What about rehearsal for your musical? After all,
         it is Tuesday!

         SELMA looks up.

SELMA   So it is.

JEFF   But maybe you're not in the mood?

         SELMA smiles at him.

SELMA   Sure I am! Always!

         JEFF starts the engine.

INT./EXT. REHEARSAL ROOM – NIGHT

         *Rehearsals are underway when JEFF and
         SELMA arrive. BORIS and SUZAN dance
         together, along with several others. SAMUEL
         directs. Behind the PIANIST, a little GIRL sits,
         holding a pair of drumsticks. A whisper spreads
         when they spot SELMA. All activity ceases.
         The piano music halts. SAMUEL steps bashfully
         to the edge of the stage.*

SAMUEL   Hello, Selma.

SELMA   Hi, Samuel.

SAMUEL   We weren't sure you'd show up.

SELMA   Sure I showed up! But I don't think this is my
          scene.

SAMUEL   No, but we can do your scene if you like.

SELMA   No, don't worry. I'll just sit and watch for a while.

          *SAMUEL nods and goes back to the others. He
          talks to them quietly while SELMA sits down near
          the back. SAMUEL cues the piano player, but
          nobody makes much of an effort. Most just stare
          at SELMA. SAMUEL steps backstage and makes
          a phone call. We can't hear him, but he nods and
          gazes gravely into the auditorium. He comes back
          on stage and steps down to where SELMA is
          sitting. Her attention is on the stage and the
          music. Few people try to complete the scene.
          Now SELMA is troubled.*

SELMA   *(turns to Jeff)* Maybe we should leave?
          Gene might wonder where I am...

SAMUEL   *(quickly)* No. Selma, just stay here. Gene knows
          this is where you go on Tuesdays.

          *SELMA nods. She sits there for a while. Then she
          gets up.*

SELMA   No, I must be going, Samuel. He hasn't seen me
all day. I don't want him to be frightened!
(looks at SAMUEL)
I'll come back another day. When you're doing
my scene…

SAMUEL But, we were just about to do your scene, Selma.
Your tapping scene…

*He turns quickly towards the stage. He claps his
hands.*

SAMUEL Alright, let's get ready for Selma's scene.
We haven't rehearsed it in weeks!
(he turns to SELMA)
Come on, Selma. You come from the same
convent as Maria. You're like a mother to her.
You like each other, but now she is leaving you
and your sister nuns, and you let her out of the
gate. Intro! Music!

*The piano segues from the preceding song.
SELMA thinks for a moment. Then she shakes her
head.*

SELMA   I'm sorry, Samuel, but I really must go.

SAMUEL But we've found you a drummer, Selma! Like you
wanted. And our little drummer, she's here for the
first time tonight! Come and say hi to Selma,
Betty!

SAMUEL beckons for the little GIRL with the drumsticks. She approaches the edge of the stage shyly. SELMA looks up at her. SAMUEL climbs on stage.

SAMUEL   Hey, gang, let's do the big finale with Betty and all.

SAMUEL looks at SELMA, she looks uncertain.

SAMUEL   No that's right, Selma doesn't like finales... so lets go for 'Climb ev'ry mountain'...

Everyone gets in line. Piano music and primitive drumming with sticks on a table commence.

ALL ON THE STAGE
'Climb ev'ry mountain, search high and low.
Follow every byway, every path you know.
Climb ev'ry mountain, ford every stream.
Follow every rainbow till you find your dream.'

SELMA watches the clumsy performance with its very heavy rhythm and amateur dance steps. She smiles when she hears the words and music as they sing and dance.

She sits down, her attention on the stage. SAMUEL smiles and they all dance and sing. They look at SELMA. SELMA turns to JEFF and smiles.

SELMA   They are good, right?

JEFF   They are OK…

          SELMA smiles. She closes her eyes as they sing.
          She hears only the sound of the drumsticks now.

INT./EXT. REHEARSAL ROOM – NIGHT

          Song: 'In the musicals #1'

          SELMA is in love with the dance and the song on
          the stage and soon she is up there among them
          in perfect harmony. Even JEFF takes part.

SELMA   Why do I love it so much?
          What kind of magic is this?
          How come I can't help adore it?
          It's just another musical.
          No one minds it at all
          If I'm having a ball,
          We're in a musical, a musical,
          And there's always someone to catch me,
          There's always someone for me,
          There's always someone to catch me,
          When you fall…

          As the dance peaks SELMA lets herself fall from
          the stage. Two MEN in police uniforms catch her.

INT./EXT. REHEARSAL ROOM – NIGHT

> *The song ends very abruptly (there are more verses to come). SELMA has fallen off the edge of the stage and is caught by two POLICEMEN who just arrived out back in the police car. Now that the song is over, they drag her out. SAMUEL is crying… JEFF is outraged… the whole place is in chaos.*

INT. COURT ROOM – DAY

> *SELMA sits at the defendant's table. KATHY and JEFF sit in the public gallery. LINDA is also there, along with everything else that pertains to a trial. The DEFENSE ATTORNEY sits beside SELMA. He looks tired. The DISTRICT ATTORNEY presents his opening statement.*

DISTRICT ATTORNEY

> The state will show that the accused has not only perpetrated the most callous, well-planned homicide in recent memory, but is also a fundamentally selfish individual who cynically hides behind a handicap, devoid of sympathy for anybody but herself, and is so meritorious of our contempt that the jury will convict her without hesitation, and thus open the way to a punishment so severe that it will deter any other murderers from following in her footsteps!

KATHY buries her face in her hands. SELMA looks around. Her attention is drawn to the court stenotype machine, which clatters away.

DISTRICT ATTORNEY
(points at SELMA) This woman found trust and friendship when she sought refuge in our country. The evidence will show that she has repaid such kindness with betrayal, robbery and murder, inflicted upon the very people who opened their homes and hearts to her!

The STENOGRAPHER's fingers keep pace to the DA's flurry of rhetoric.

DISTRICT ATTORNEY
Honorable members of the jury, the evidence will prove that she herself did not show that mercy she will ask of us when she tried to steal away the man who Linda Houston had been married to for 25 years! When in cold blood she robbed the Houstons of their life's savings and the wherewithal of their existence! When she inflicted on Officer Bill Houston – one of the most respected members of our community – the 34 wounds which, after inconceivable suffering, terminated his life. When she butchered him right there on his own living room floor?

SELMA is no longer listening.

INT. COURT ROOM – DAY

> *LINDA in the witness box.*

LINDA   She wanted my husband. But he didn't want her,
         so she killed him, not hesitating even when he
         pleaded for his life. 'I beg you, Selma!' he said,
         but she just kept firing—
         (begins to sob)
         He cried and pleaded for mercy. But she showed
         no mercy – and you shall be given no mercy
         either, Selma!

INT. COURT ROOM – DAY

> *FORENSIC PATHOLOGIST in witness box.*

FORENSIC PATHOLOGIST
         (nods) The most macabre corpse I have seen in
         years. The body was inhumanely battered…

INT. COURT ROOM – DAY

> *The SHOP ASSISTANT from the jewelry shop in
> the witness box.*

DISTRICT ATTORNEY
         You came forward because you heard about the
         case and knew the accused?

SHOP ASSISTANT

Yes, she ordered a number of items from
my store—

DISTRICT ATTORNEY

Cheap costume items or expensive jewelry?

SHOP ASSISTANT

Expensive. Very expensive. She was only
interested in the most expensive ones.
They made her more beautiful, she said—

DISTRICT ATTORNEY

And did you not have your doubts about
commissioning these expensive items for this
rather ordinary woman?

SHOP ASSISTANT

As a matter of fact, I did, but she gave me a real
fancy name – it sounded like she was wealthy –
like royalty or something...

DISTRICT ATTORNEY

(looks at SELMA) A false name, you say?

INT. COURT ROOM – DAY

The DOCTOR in the witness box.

DOCTOR   I examined her eyesight shortly before the
         homicide. She was myopic... that is
         shortsighted... but nothing special; and stable.
         I understand that her eye condition has
         complicated since then.

INT. COURT ROOM – DAY

         LINDA replies to the DEFENSE ATTORNEY.

LINDA   She asked me about the money, in great detail.
         And she wanted to be sure where he kept his
         revolver in the house.

INT. COURT ROOM – DAY

         A POLICE DETECTIVE in the witness box.

DETECTIVE
         We found the bag from the Savings and Loan, but
         not the money.

DISTRICT ATTORNEY
         And was it the bag Bill Houston kept in his
         deposit box at the Savings and Loan?

DETECTIVE
         The very same – Houston's blood was all over it.

DISTRICT ATTORNEY
> And how is it linked to the accused?

DETECTIVE
> We found it in the forest where the witness
> testifies he drove the accused on the day of the
> homicide.

DISTRICT ATTORNEY
> If the accused had concealed the money in the
> forest, would you say that it was possible, or not
> possible that somebody else found it and
> emptied the bag?

DETECTIVE
> Possible. It's more like a park really. Quite a lot of
> people go there.

DISTRICT ATTORNEY
> *(nods and turns to SELMA, who is dreaming)*
> Thank you. I am happy that people like you are
> prepared to help us clarify all these mysteries –
> since the accused is not inclined to do so—

INT. COURT ROOM – DAY

> *NORMAN in the witness box.*

DISTRICT ATTORNEY
> And although our great country took her in as a

refugee, she had nothing but contempt for our
system of government?

NORMAN *(leans over)* She said communism was better for
human beings – apart from – health care…

DISTRICT ATTORNEY
(nods) She left her beloved communist state
not out of any desire for freedom, or out of love
for our country and its principles, but to derive
advantage from the advances made by
American medical personnel – to do nothing less
than exploit our costly health care system for her
own ends – and yet you say the accused was a
loyal worker?

NORMAN She was a fine co-worker—

DISTRICT ATTORNEY
But not so fine that in the end you had to fire her
because she failed to do her job properly?

NORMAN Yes, that's true. She used to day-dream—

DISTRICT ATTORNEY
Used to think of herself, in other words.
But after all, she had not come to America to
work; she had come to America to enjoy its
medical science!

NORMAN *(thinks, and then brightens)* Yes, and its musicals!
The American ones were better, she said—

DISTRICT ATTORNEY
(sarcastically) Its musicals too? So the accused
preferred Hollywood to Vladivostok? Well, I
suppose it's an acknowledgement of sorts…
Musicals? So this nation has made some
contribution at least!

INT. COURT ROOM – DAY

*SELMA has taken the stand. The DISTRICT
ATTORNEY questions her.*

DISTRICT ATTORNEY
Your sight was poor, you claim; indeed, we have
heard as much from your best friend – contrary to
the expert testimony we have received. But you
saw well enough to inflict 34 wounds on Bill
Houston. Why did you kill him, actually? If I may
have the temerity to ask?

SELMA He wanted me to.

DISTRICT ATTORNEY
He did? How intriguing! A man with a fine career,
some wealth, and a happy marriage? Why would
this Bill Houston want you to kill him?

SELMA   I promised him I wouldn't say.

DISTRICT ATTORNEY
        Ah, that clears things up immensely! You
        promised you wouldn't say! In that case we'll just
        have to take your word for it when you say that
        the money you stole was your own, despite the
        fact that Bill Houston's savings also disappeared
        so mysteriously that very day? And just where did
        you get your money?

SELMA   I'd been saving up.

DISTRICT ATTORNEY
        I suppose you might call it that… and what were
        these savings to be spent on? You never bought
        your son so much as a single birthday present, as
        we've heard.

SELMA   *(looks at KATHY)* On—

DISTRICT ATTORNEY
        Yes? Come on, out with it! I'm afraid the jury
        demands some sort of answer!

SELMA   *(quickly)* On – my father in Czechoslovakia.
        I sent him money…

DISTRICT ATTORNEY
        To your father? And what, pray tell, is his name?

SELMA   *(uncertainly)* My father? His name is Oldrich Nový.

DISTRICT ATTORNEY
         Thank you! We are meant to believe that you
         killed Bill Houston by inflicting 34 wounds on him
         because he asked you to; as we are meant to
         believe you were blind when you did it; as we are
         meant to believe that it was your own savings
         that you stole from him – just as we are meant to
         believe that every month you sent all you had to
         your father back home, a man by the name of
         Oldrich Nový? Is this so?

SELMA   *(hesitates, then nods)* Yes, it is so.

DISTRICT ATTORNEY
         Thank you, Ms. Jezková.

         SELMA leaves the chair.

INT. COURT ROOM – DAY

         *The DISTRICT ATTORNEY walks towards
         the jury.*

DISTRICT ATTORNEY
         Honorable members of the jury! You have now
         heard from the accused's own lips. You must
         believe her, just as you must believe her when
         she claims her father's name is Oldrich Nový.

He looks at judge.

DISTRICT ATTORNEY

Your Honor, at this time the State calls to the
witness stand, Oldrich Nový!

*SELMA looks up. An OLDER MAN walks in.
Hand on the Bible, he is sworn in.*

DISTRICT ATTORNEY

Would you please state your full name?

OLDER MAN

(in poor English) My name is Oldrich Nový.

DISTRICT ATTORNEY

You used to live in Czechoslovakia?

OLDRICH NOVÝ

Yes. Now I live in California. As you know.

DISTRICT ATTORNEY

Yes, that's where we found you. Do you know of
any other Oldrich Nový in Czechoslovakia?

OLDRICH NOVÝ

No. I have never heard of any…

DISTRICT ATTORNEY

And surely you would if any! So tell me, what is
your relation to the accused?

OLDRICH NOVÝ looks briefly at SELMA.

OLDRICH NOVÝ
>   I do not know her.

DISTRICT ATTORNEY
>   You don't know her! So you have not received
>   money from her every month, money that she
>   says was so dearly earned?

OLDRICH NOVÝ
>   No.

DISTRICT ATTORNEY
>   Perhaps you are not her father then?

OLDRICH NOVÝ
>   Indeed, no.

DISTRICT ATTORNEY
>   If the relationship is imagined by the accused,
>   would there be any way of her knowing your
>   name?

OLDRICH NOVÝ
>   I was well-known in Czechoslovakia in my time.
>   She is sure to know me from when she was a
>   child... because of my profession...

DISTRICT ATTORNEY
>   Yes, and Mr. Oldrich Nový, what is your

profession? Perhaps that can give us a clue to why this maybe somewhat romantic, certainly communistic woman – who worships Fred Astaire but not his country – could have lied and misused your name, to make everybody believe that all her money was spent on a poor father and not her own vanity?

OLDRICH NOVÝ

I am an actor... I made these films... They were very popular. Also in the countryside and among the young. I used to sing and dance... mostly tap... it was... musicals!

SELMA closes her eyes. She is drifting away to the rhythm of the stenotype machine.

INT. COURT ROOM – DAY

Song: 'In the musicals #2'

SELMA is in love with her childhood hero. She sings to him and finally succeeds in getting him to tap with her on the judge's table. It turns into a kind of duel, SELMA doing her best, but NOVÝ outdoes her every time. By the end of the tap sequence she only stamps her feet in an effort to make him show her more and more. Then they all dance along in this large-scale setup.

SELMA   *(looking at NOVÝ)*
         Why do I love you so much?
         What kind of magic is it?
         How come I can't help adore you?
         You were in a musical.
         You didn't mind it at all
         That I was having a ball,
         At your musical, your musical!
         And you were always there to catch me,
         You were always there for me,
         You were always there to catch me,
         When I'd fall...

         Tap duel

SELMA   Say it again!

OLDRIC NOVÝ
         I don't mind it at all
         If you're having a ball,
         This is a musical, a musical!
         I'll always be there to catch you,
         I'll always be there for you,
         I'll always be there to catch you,
         When you fall...

EVERYBODY
         In the musicals, the musicals!
         We'll always be there to catch you,
         We'll always be there for you,
         We'll always be there to catch you,

When you fall...
In the musicals, the musicals!
We'll always be there to catch you,
We'll always be there for you,
We'll always be there to catch you,
When you fall...

*The song is interrupted at its peak by the
OFFICER OF THE COURT's line.*

INT. COURT ROOM – DAY

OFFICER OF THE COURT
    Will the court please rise!

*Everybody rises. The JURY sits down. Everyone
else follows suit.*

JUDGE   *(to the FOREMAN of the JURY)*
    Have you reached a verdict?

FOREMAN Yes, your honor.

*The FOREMAN hands a piece of paper to the
OFFICER OF THE COURT, who conveys it to the
JUDGE. He puts on his glasses and reads it. Then
he hands it down to the CLERK OF COURT.*

CLERK OF COURT
    (reads aloud) We, the jury, find the accused,

Selma Jezková, guilty of murder in the first
degree...

KATHY closes her eyes.

CLERK OF COURT
...and sentence her hereby to death!

*KATHY utters a little scream. SELMA looks
around as if she doesn't really understand. We
focus exclusively on SELMA, KATHY, and JEFF.*

JUDGE   *(off, to FOREMAN of the JURY)* Is this the verdict
of this jury? You fully understand that it must be
unanimous?

FOREMAN *(off)* Yes, your honor.

JUDGE   *(off)* Selma Jezková, you are hereby sentenced to
be taken from this place and confined in the state
penitentiary until such time as you shall be
executed by being hung from the neck until you
are dead.

The JUDGE brings down his gavel.

EXT. STATE PENITENTIARY – WINTER/EVENING

*Winter storm. We move through the gale with
KATHY as she walks down the noisy city streets,*

and into a huge, modern top-security prison. We
can tell that KATHY has been this way before.

INT. STATE PENITENTIARY/VISITORS' ROOM –
WINTER/EVENING

Now KATHY sits in the silent isolation-block
visitor's room. She waits. SELMA is brought in;
she wears inmate's overalls and is in handcuffs.
BRENDA, a GUARD, settles SELMA in a chair,
then moves a short distance away, where she
monitors KATHY's visit. SELMA sits opposite
KATHY, a sheet of plate glass between them.
They sit there for awhile. KATHY looks at
SELMA, concerned.

KATHY   How you doing, Selma?

SELMA   Oh, you know – I'm doing just fine.

KATHY   I'm so sorry about the supreme court decision.

SELMA   Yes, I just heard about it. It's not very pleasant.

KATHY sits there a moment.

KATHY   Aren't you gonna ask how he is?

SELMA looks down. KATHY looks at her defiantly.

KATHY   Gene's fine, Selma, besides the fact he's not able to see his mother.

KATHY looks urgently at SELMA.

KATHY   Gene wants to visit so bad. Won't you let him see you now? Please?

SELMA   *(sits for a while, struggles with her emotions, shakes her head)* There's nothing for him to see! He's got you now, Kathy. I know you're looking after him. I don't even have to ask about that, because I just know you are.

KATHY   May I give him your love, at least?

SELMA   The sooner he gets used to being on his own the better. He should spend his time on looking to the future, not dreaming that things could be different. He has a life of his own to live. I will never be a part of that. He has just got to understand that now.

KATHY   You're a hard woman, Selma.

SELMA   Well…

KATHY   They said you'd asked to see me?

SELMA   *(nods)* Yes, that's right. Some practical stuff.

KATHY   Yes, Selma? What is it?

SELMA   On his birthday, Gene will receive a letter from
          me. I want you to make sure he reads it and does
          what it says. As I probably won't be here then.

KATHY   Okay.

SELMA   *(frowns)* He is to take it seriously and do just what
          it says and not be afraid because there is nothing
          to be afraid of! Do you promise you'll get him to
          understand that?

KATHY   Sure, Selma, I promise.

SELMA   Thank you, Kathy. You are a real friend.

          *They sit there awhile. BRENDA looks at her
          watch.*

BRENDA   Time's up, Selma.

          *SELMA nods. She gets up. Something occurs to
          her. She turns to KATHY.*

SELMA   And he is to call himself Nový! That is very
          important. I know it sounds foolish, but he has to.
          I didn't dare tell you before, in case they wrecked
          everything. But since the case is closed, I don't
          think it matters any more.

KATHY   *(puzzled)* Why should he call himself Nový?

SELMA   *(smiles and looks at KATHY through her blind eyes)*
           Stop asking so many questions, Cvalda! I'll write
           all about it in my letter – so you'll remember.

KATHY   *(looks at her seriously)* Can I give him your love
           then… please!

SELMA   *(shakes her head)* No.

           *BRENDA takes SELMA away. KATHY is left there,
           looking grave.*

**INT. STATE PENITENTIARY, ISOLATION ROW –
EVENING**

           *BRENDA leads SELMA down the corridor to her
           cell. SELMA is crying silent tears.*

BRENDA   You love your son very much, Selma, I know.

SELMA   *(nods)* Yes, I do.

BRENDA   I got a boy of my own back home.

SELMA   You do? You never told me.

BRENDA   No, but anyhow, I know what it is to have a son.

They reach SELMA's cell on isolation row.
BRENDA lets SELMA in. She locks the door again
and opens the Judas hole. SELMA turns, well-
practiced, and puts her wrists through the hole.
BRENDA undoes her handcuffs, removes them.

BRENDA   G'night, Selma, I go off duty in 15 minutes.
          Sleep tight – it'll soon be lights out.

SELMA   *(smiles from her side of the door)*
          They needn't turn them off for my sake.

BRENDA   *(embarrassed)* I'm sorry, Selma, I forgot. I didn't
          mean to make fun of you.

SELMA   No, Brenda, I know you didn't. Goodnight,
          Brenda. You sleep tight too, and say hello to your
          boy for me.

BRENDA   I'll do that.

          BRENDA shuts the Judas hole and goes. SELMA
          is alone in the sterile, modern cell.

INT. JEFF'S PICK-UP – DAY/WINTER

          JEFF drives through the forest. He pulls in
          opposite the bus stop we saw earlier. He gets out
          and looks across the field.

EXT. FOREST – DAY/WINTER

> JEFF walks through the forest, along the path that SELMA followed. He passes the bench and the lake. He reaches the sign without words where the path goes off in several directions. He stands there for a moment, not knowing which way to go. A BOY walks towards him with a white cane. The BOY finds the blank sign with his cane. He feels the raised arrow, and sets off down the narrow path. JEFF watches him go, then sets off after him.

INT. HOSPITAL – DAY/WINTER

> JEFF passes a reception building. Inside, there is a RECEPTIONIST in white. She peers through the half-window at JEFF. He looks around.

RECEPTIONIST
> Can I help you? Are you looking for someone?

JEFF *(hesitating)* Oh, I'm not really sure…

RECEPTIONIST
> Are you looking for a patient?

JEFF Maybe somebody who was a patient once.
Do you have a list?

RECEPTIONIST
>Only if it wasn't too long ago. What's the
>patient's name?

JEFF   Jezková. Selma Jezková.

>*The RECEPTIONIST checks various records.*
>*She shakes her head.*

RECEPTIONIST
>No, I'm sorry. I can't find that name.

JEFF   Hey, that's too bad. Thanks for your help.

>*JEFF is about to go. Then he stops.*

JEFF   What about Nový? Maybe you've got a Nový
>in your records somewhere?

INT. STATE PENITENTIARY/VISITORS' ROOM – DAY

>*KATHY sits in the visitor's chair opposite SELMA,*
>*who is on the other side of the plate glass.*
>*KATHY looks expectantly at her. KATHY smiles.*

KATHY   I've got good news for you!

SELMA   What's that?

KATHY   We've located a new attorney. He says he can

	get your case reopened. He says your old attorney was incompetent.
SELMA	*(sits there a moment)* Is this true?
KATHY	Yes, and he thinks he can get the death penalty commuted.
SELMA	How could he do that?
KATHY	*(secretively)* New information has turned up...
SELMA	*(suspiciously)* What information?
KATHY	We know the whole story, Selma. That you spent your money for Gene's operation.
SELMA	How do you know that?
KATHY	Jeff found the hospital and talked to the doctor. Selma, why didn't you say anything?
SELMA	Have you told Gene?
KATHY	No...
SELMA	That's good. He must not know until it is time. It's very important!
KATHY	*(frowns, and ponders)* Listen. Don't you see that it would help the jury to know that you were trying

	to stop your son from going blind? Then they might believe the money was your own savings.
SELMA	*(thinks)* If he gets worse from worrying, the operation might not make his eyes good…
KATHY	*(ignoring her)* The attorney thinks you've a much better case now! Maybe you'll get manslaughter instead... he needs to finish a case – and then he'll come and see you... in two weeks' time.
SELMA	*(Wakes up, shakes her head)* But it's next week—
KATHY	We know that, but he says you just have to apply for a stay. The vast majority of cases get one the first time.
SELMA	Is that so?
KATHY	So will you?
SELMA	Will I what?
KATHY	Apply for a stay so we can get the case reopened?

SELMA begins to cry. She pulls herself together and nods.

| SELMA | I'm sorry, I'm just so happy! |

INT. STATE PENITENTIARY ISOLATION ROW – NIGHT

> *SELMA sits in her cell. BRENDA enters. She sits down opposite SELMA.*

BRENDA   They haven't phoned yet! But there's still plenty of time.

SELMA   If they don't phone, what then?

BRENDA   You'll be transferred to a cell in the other block sometime tomorrow.

SELMA   The block where they hang people?

BRENDA   Yes – where they spend the last day.

SELMA   *(sadly)* And then they have to go the 136 steps...

BRENDA   They told you that?

SELMA   And won't you be there, Brenda?

BRENDA   No, I work over here, but Selma, it's certain they'll grant a stay... I can't imagine you not getting one.

SELMA   I'm worried all the same. The waiting is so unpleasant.

BRENDA   Of course it is. Can't you try thinking of something nice?

SELMA   *(shakes her head sadly)* Not with it being so
         quiet here!

BRENDA   What's that got to do with it?

SELMA   *(smiles)* At the factory I could dream I was in a
         musical and that the machinery was the music –
         in musicals nothing dreadful ever happens – and
         then I could take just about anything! But it's so
         quiet here. I thought in prisons people marched
         about!

         BRENDA smiles.

BRENDA   No, there's not much noise around here.

SELMA   *(smiles furtively)* But a bit later they'll turn on
         the radio.

BRENDA   There's no radio in the isolation block.

SELMA   If I listen to the pipes I can hear someone
         singing. Hymns. I heard it yesterday.
         Somewhat later, it was...

         SELMA is suddenly troubled.

SELMA   I mean, if listening to the pipes isn't against the
         rules—

BRENDA *(smiles)* No. No, it isn't. It will be singing from the
        chapel you hear. There must be a sermon.
        You just listen away, Selma.

INT. STATE PENITENTIARY ISOLATION ROW – NIGHT

*SELMA sits on her cot, listening to the pipe.
At first it's silent, but then religious music is
heard, very faintly. SELMA smiles. There's music.
She shuts her eyes.*

INT. STATE PENITENTIARY ISOLATION ROW – NIGHT

Song: 'My favorite things'

*Alone in her cell SELMA is putting the song
she learned on top of the sounds from the mass.
This song is her strongest weapon against the
present danger.*

SELMA   'Raindrops on roses and whiskers on kittens,
        Bright copper kettles and warm woolen mittens,
        Brown paper packages tied up with strings,
        These are a few of my favorite things.
        Creamed colored ponies and crisp apple strudels,
        Doorbells and sleighbells and schnitzel with noodles,
        Wild geese that fly with the moon on their wings,
        These are a few of my favorite things.
        Girls in white dresses with blue satin sashes,

Snowflakes that stay on my nose and eyelashes,
Silver white winters that melt into springs,
These are a few of my favorite things.'

INT. STATE PENITENTIARY ISOLATION ROW – NIGHT

*Cross-cut to BRENDA, who passes SELMA's cell
at one stage, outside SELMA's dream. She looks
at the rapturous, smiling SELMA listening to the
pipe. BRENDA is touched by her joy.*

INT. STATE PENITENTIARY ISOLATION ROW – NIGHT

Song: 'My favorite things' cont.

SELMA   'When the dog bites, when the bee stings, when
I'm feeling sad,
I simply remember my favorite things, and then I
don't feel so bad!'

INT. STATE PENITENTIARY ISOLATION ROW – NIGHT

*Then BRENDA goes inside and brings SELMA
back gently. SELMA wakes up. BRENDA smiles
at her.*

BRENDA   You got your stay, Selma! I'm sure everything will
work out fine! Just fine!

The news has to sink in first, and then SELMA hugs BRENDA, crying heavily.

INT. STATE PENITENTIARY/OFFICIAL VISITORS' ROOM – DAY

> *SELMA is conducted into this somewhat brighter room by BRENDA. There is even a window, and beyond it, daylight. There's a table and two chairs. On one chair sits the new ATTORNEY. He gets up and offers his hand to SELMA.*

NEW DEFENSE COUNSEL
> I'm your new legal counsel, Selma.

> *BRENDA withdraws. The ATTORNEY helps SELMA onto her chair.*

NEW DEFENSE COUNSEL
> I'm quite sure we can have your sentence commuted. All I need is your signature saying you want the case reopened. I'll have all the paperwork ready by tomorrow.

SELMA *(smiles)* That sounds wonderful!

NEW DEFENSE COUNSEL
> *(smiles)* We'll win the jury over, you'll see! The fact that you were fighting for your son is something

we can really push. I've plenty of experience in
cases like this!

SELMA   The other attorney had, too, he said...

NEW DEFENSE COUNSEL
         (gets out new papers) Yes, but he was appointed
         by the court. And you don't get the best counsel
         that way...

SELMA   *(troubled)* So you were not appointed by the
         court?

NEW DEFENCE COUNSEL
         No. I'm sorry to say that I will have to charge
         you for my services. But that's all taken care of.
         I've made a deal with your ladyfriend.

SELMA   A deal?

NEW DEFENSE COUNSEL
         Yes, in regard to my fee. I've accepted the
         amount she said she could raise.

SELMA   *(warily)* And how much was that?

NEW DEFENSE COUNSEL
         (with a smile) Well, I can tell you precisely,
         because I received an envelope. 2000 dollars
         and...

SELMA   2056 dollars... and 10 cents?

NEW DEFENSE COUNSEL
        (surprised) Yes, that's precisely right.

        SELMA nods. She sits there for a moment,
        suddenly distant again.

NEW DEFENSE COUNSEL
        Shall we review our tactics? I have a couple of
        questions...

        SELMA does not respond.

INT. STATE PENITENTIARY/VISITORS' ROOM – DAY

        KATHY sits happily on her chair, waiting for
        SELMA. SELMA is led in. She is angry.

SELMA   That was Gene's money! The money you gave to
         the attorney!

KATHY   *(understands)* We thought saving your life was
         more important.

SELMA   It's Gene's money!

KATHY   Then we'll just have to find money for Gene later.

SELMA   It's now he needs it. He's 13 next month!

KATHY   Money will turn up some way or another.

SELMA   *(shakes her head)* Don't you see? Can't I trust
        my own friends any more? What stupidity,
        spending that kind of money on a blind
        woman who'll only spend the rest of her life
        in prison!

KATHY   Gene wants his mother – alive – no matter where!
        If you plan to take his mother away from him…
        I am not your friend anymore!

SELMA   I want you to give Gene that money for his
        operation, just like you promised! I've been
        saving up since the day he was born! He didn't
        ask to be born with his mother's sick eyes!
        Every night I have promised myself that one day,
        Gene would be able to see his grandchildren.

KATHY   *(gets cross)* If that money is not used to get your
        death sentence commuted, I'll throw it into the
        ocean! And I'll make sure Gene never gets his
        operation! I mean it, Selma! Listen to reason…
        for once!

SELMA   I listen to my heart.

        KATHY gets into a rage.

KATHY   You are so stupid! I'll tell you what I'll do… I will
        tell the police about the money… I will tell them it

is the money you stole from Bill. Then they will
take the money away…

KATHY gets up angrily and walks out.
SELMA sits there for a moment; then
BRENDA fetches her.

INT. STATE PENITENTIARY/OFFICIAL VISITORS' ROOM – DAY

SELMA is brought in to meet her new counsel.
She takes her chair without help. He is about to
say hello, but she interrupts.

SELMA   Is the deal with my ladyfriend the kind that can
be terminated without costing anything? I mean,
can I have my money back?

NEW DEFENSE COUNSEL
        (surprised) I can get you a retrial, and I can get
you a lighter sentence, Selma. It's not just
make-believe.

SELMA   Can we have the money back?

NEW DEFENSE COUNSEL
        (thinks) If you have changed your mind… then—

SELMA   Then I want my son to have that money back!

NEW DEFENSE COUNSEL
>   *(sits for a moment)* You do realize what will
>   happen?

SELMA   *(nods)* I've already told them I don't want any
>   more stays!

>   *The ATTORNEY looks at her.*

SELMA   *(calmly)* No more stays of execution.
>   That is my decision!

>   *The ATTORNEY nods.*

EXT. STATE PENITENTIARY – DAY

>   *The street is decked out with Christmas
>   decorations.*

INT. STATE PENITENTIARY/VISITORS' ROOM – DAY

>   *SELMA waits. She looks tiny but relaxed. JEFF is
>   conducted into the room by a guard. He sits
>   down on the other side of the plate glass. SELMA
>   doesn't notice him. He looks at her for a while.*

JEFF   Howdy, Selma!

>   *SELMA wakes up at the sound of his voice.*

She smiles.

SELMA   Hi, Jeff!

They don't know how to begin.

JEFF   Gene says thank you for the comics... for his
        birthday...

SELMA   *(surprised)* I didn't send him any comics!

JEFF   *(knows that he said something stupid, feels
        uneasy)* No, we bought him some. We said it was
        from you.

        *SELMA looks down. She doesn't say anything.
        JEFF looks at her and feels bad.*

JEFF   I'm sorry. It was a stupid thing to do. I knew you
        would be upset. I'm really sorry, Selma!

        *SELMA sits for a while. Then she turn her face up
        towards him again. She smiles a little.*

SELMA   I'm glad you are here, Jeff.

JEFF   I had hoped it would be different... you and me...

SELMA   Yes, but that was not to be—
        (worried that she has hurt him)
        Not that you aren't a good man, because you are!

It was me… You were the best that could have happened to me… Truly…

JEFF   *(nods a little, turns serious)* Gene wanted to be there when it happens, but they said no.
           He is too young…

SELMA   *(pretending to be angry)* That's good. Who ever put that crazy idea into his head?

JEFF   *(gathers his courage)* I'll be there instead…
           If you want me to…

SELMA   And Kathy?

JEFF   I don't think so, Selma. She's still pissed…
           you know her.

SELMA   *(smiles)* Yes… yes I do. It's kind of you, Jeff… if you think you can take it… yes, I would be very happy if you would be there…

           They sit quietly for a moment.

JEFF   Is there anything you want to ask me, Selma?

SELMA   No… I don't think so?

JEFF   About Gene… or anything…

SELMA   *(nods)* No, no… it's out of my hands now.

He's living with Kathy… that couldn't be better…
she's pissed now… but she's my friend…

JEFF   And you still don't want to see him… or talk on
the phone? There is time for that, you know…
it would make him real happy…

SELMA   *(smiles)* I doubt that it would make anybody
real happy.

*JEFF sits for a while. Then he straightens up in
the chair.*

JEFF   I will go now, Selma.

SELMA   Yes, it was nice of you to come. Goodbye Jeff.

JEFF   Goodbye, Selma. You are a beautiful lady.

JEFF gets up. Then he stops.

JEFF   Why did you do it? Why did you have Gene,
when you knew he would have your eyes?

She shakes her head.

SELMA   I've no excuse, Jeff!

*JEFF looks at the tormented SELMA with
great pity.*

SELMA *(hunches up and speaks very quietly)* I just so
    much wanted to hold a little baby in my arms.

    Tears are running down SELMA's cheeks now.
    JEFF looks at her with mute compassion.

INT. STATE PENITENTIARY/ISOLATION ROW – NIGHT

    SELMA sits restlessly in her cell. BRENDA arrives
    with two other guards. She knocks.

BRENDA It's time, Selma.

    SELMA gets up and turns her back to the Judas
    hole so BRENDA can cuff her. BRENDA opens
    the door.

BRENDA Goodbye, Selma.

SELMA Goodbye, Brenda.

    The two GUARDS lead SELMA away down the
    corridor. BRENDA watches her go.

INT. STATE PENITENTIARY DEATH ROW WITH TWO CELLS – NIGHT

    The two GUARDS conduct SELMA into one of
    the cells. They help her to sit down on the bare

mattress. Then they let themselves out. SELMA
sits on the bed as if turned to stone. She listens,
but there isn't a sound.

INT. STATE PENITENTIARY DEATH ROW WITH TWO CELLS – NIGHT

SELMA's last meal is being served... It's a
hamburger with fries from the kitchen.

GUARD   Your meal, Jezková!

SELMA nods, but otherwise ignores the meal.

INT. STATE PENITENTIARY DEATH ROW WITH TWO CELLS/CORRIDOR AND GALLOWS CHAMBER – NIGHT

SELMA lies on the mattress, awake, blind eyes
wide open. She hears somebody coming. She
closes her eyes; she does not want it to be now.
She takes a deep breath.

SELMA   Is it now?

GUARD   *(off)* Yeah, it's now.

The GUARD has arrived with some OFFICIALS.

SELMA   Good.

            The GUARD opens the door with all its handles.
            SELMA gets up with difficulty.

SELMA   I'm sorry. But I'm a bit nervous.

            She tries to move her feet, but they don't
            really work...

SELMA   *(whispers sadly)* I don't think I can walk...

            Two of the GUARDS step in and lift her up.

BRENDA   *(off)* She can walk on her own!

            BRENDA is one of the little group in the corridor.

SELMA   *(surprised)* Brenda! I didn't think you worked here!

            BRENDA is in her ordinary clothes, not her
            prison garb.

BRENDA   I don't. But they let me come. I asked to be
            allowed...

SELMA   Oh, thank you. I'm so pleased you came!
            But I am afraid that I will have to disappoint
            you... I am not so brave. My legs really don't
            work well today...

144

BRENDA   You can do it, Selma.

SELMA   136 steps. I can't do one!

Two of the GUARDS look at BRENDA.

BRENDA   I'll be next to you... I thought I could be here and
make you some sound. If I march... you'd have
something to listen to... remember?

BRENDA stamps her feet in a rhythm.
SELMA listens.

SELMA   (smiles and shakes her head) But Brenda...

BRENDA   No, Selma... just listen! Come on, you can do it!

SELMA considers. She listens to BRENDA's
stamping. She closes her eyes and concentrates
on the sound. She manages a step. But it is very
difficult.

BRENDA   That's one...

One of the other wardens helps BRENDA with the
stamping. SELMA starts to move. On the way
down the corridor, other staff members seem to
fall in too.

BRENDA   ...two, three...

> *SELMA smiles. She can do it. The rhythm is*
> *pronounced now.*

INT. STATE PENITENTIARY DEATH ROW WITH TWO CELLS/CORRIDOR AND GALLOWS CHAMBER – NIGHT

> *Song: 'The 136 steps'*

BRENDA (Counts all the way from 4 to 135.)

SELMA   (Counts now and then.)

ALL   (Count in the end until 135.)

> *SELMA is on her way, helped by her music. She*
> *dips in and out of cells on the way, but is always*
> *coming back to the leading BRENDA. Just before*
> *the execution chamber the prison looks suddenly*
> *more like a zoo, with big, surrealistic caves*
> *around the corridor, where inmates are living*
> *high in the air, on bars like monkeys.*

INT. STATE PENITENTIARY/GALLOWS CHAMBER – NIGHT

> *Suddenly before the last number everything*
> *becomes quiet. '136' is heard with only SELMA's*
> *fragile voice. SELMA is in the gallows chamber.*

She is standing on the trap door. Everybody is
quiet now. She wakes up. Then she realizes
where she is. She looks around like an animal
catching a scent. She is puzzled. Down to her
left are the witnesses sitting in the half darkness.
A MAN steps up to her with the hood. SELMA
feels him near and falls down on the floor.

BRENDA   *(in pain)* Selma, you have to stand...

SELMA   *(down to the floor)* I'm sorry... I'm so sorry...

BRENDA   Try to stand, Selma...

SELMA can't. Two GUARDS are coming up to her
carrying the 'collapse board'.

BRENDA   *(with no conviction)* She can stand... You don't
have to do that.

The GUARDS are placing SELMA on the wooden
board. They strap her to it with the leather straps.
SELMA is sobbing. The GUARDS are in light
panic. They place the board on the trapdoor.
It looks grotesque. BRENDA is heartbroken.
The MAN with the noose is not feeling good.
He puts it on SELMA's neck. It is difficult because
of the board. He forces her head violently forward
in order to do it. The MAN with the hood shakes
his head.

147

MAN WITH HOOD
> The hood...!

> *The MAN with the noose is in doubt if he should take it off again in order to place the hood first.*

SELMA   *(in a panic)* A hood... nobody has said anything about a hood...

BRENDA   *(completely broken)* It's so you don't see, Selma...

SELMA   *(tearful)* Nobody said anything about a hood. I can't breathe. Why do I have to have a hood on... I am scared, Brenda!

BRENDA   *(gets angry and looks at the others)* She can't see anything anyhow! Do you have to put that damn hood on? She's blind! Don't you realize?

> *BRENDA grabs the hood and walks angrily up to the officer responsible for the execution.*

BRENDA   She's blind, for Christ's sake!

> *The OFFICER considers.*

OFFICER I'll have to call...

> *The OFFICER phones from the other room. The execution process is thrown off track; confusion*

SELMA | spreads. SELMA is in a rage of despair.
She screams.

SELMA | Gene! Gene!

*The GUARD down by the door that leads from
the witness area to the stairs leading to the
gallows leaves his post to talk to another GUARD.
KATHY is down there. She gets up from her chair.
She is tormented by SELMA's crying. KATHY runs
towards the door to the stairs. She manages to
slip up the stairs.*

SELMA | (trying to free herself from the straps) Gene…
GENE!!!!

KATHY forces her way to SELMA. She hugs her.

KATHY | He is just outside! Gene is just outside…

SELMA | Kathy?

SELMA smiles and doesn't believe it.

KATHY | I have something for you from him…

*KATHY is violently pulled back from SELMA by a
GUARD, but she has just time to put something in
SELMA's hands. SELMA feels it. It's GENE's
glasses. SELMA freezes. She is moved.*

SELMA   *(quietly)* He's had the operation—!

KATHY   *(smiles and shouts)* He will see his grandchildren,
         Selma! And he is just outside... he is close to
         you, Selma...

         She stands there a moment, nodding happily.
         She smiles.

SELMA   Gene...

KATHY   You were right Selma... listen to your heart... you
         were so right... listen to your heart...

         Back in the office, OFFICIALS still discuss the
         hood. SELMA's mind wanders off. Motionless,
         she tries to listen. Now she hears her heart. She
         smiles at its pulse, its steady, rhythmic sound.

INT. STATE PENITENTIARY/GALLOWS CHAMBER –
NIGHT

         Song: 'The next-to-last song'

         SELMA moves into the song with complete
         confidence. Happy and exalted as never before!
         She makes up the song as she sings it with great
         pleasure. This song is filmed both in the same
         way as the other dance numbers, with the many
         fixed cameras, and with the traditional handle

camera. When we are in the fixed camera state,
everybody in the room seems to have frozen and
does not move much. In the handle camera state,
BRENDA's argument with the officials still goes
on, as does the other chaotic action.

SELMA   Oh Gene! Of course you are near,
And now there's nothing to fear,
Yes Gene, I see that you're here!
Oooooo – and I should have known
Oooooo – I was never alone
Oooooo...
They say it's the last song
They don't know us, you see,
It's only the last song
If we let it be
'The next-to-the-last-song'
Is for you – for me!
You – and me!
No matter what I have sung
Or if the tunes came out wrong
Or you complained they were long
Oooooo – the words have all been
Oooooo – I love you, dear Gene.
Oooooo...
Remember what I have said
Remember wrap up the bread,
Do this, do that; make your bed.
Oooooooo – they can't hurt us now
Oooooooo – you'll live and know how
Oooooooo...

They say it's the last song
They don't know us, you see,
It's 'The next-to-the-last-song'
If we let it be
'The next-to-the-last-song'
For you – for me!
You and…

**INT. STATE PENITENTIARY/GALLOWS CHAMBER –
NIGHT**

> In a dizzying rush, the trap door opens with a
> terrifying crash that puts an irrevocable stop to
> all song.

> SELMA's body spins. There is a dreadful sound as
> her fall is arrested by the rope around her neck.
> Her neck snaps. There is silence. SELMA dangles
> lifelessly at the end of the rope. Everyone
> watches mutely. The WARDEN comes down the
> stairs with the DOCTOR. The curtains are drawn.
> The DOCTOR puts the stethoscope to SELMA's
> chest. He listens. An OFFICER comes in and puts
> the hood on her. The DOCTOR listens to the
> increasingly spasmodic, fragile heartbeat. He
> shakes his head at the OFFICER. Everyone is
> silent now.

> We cut to an image of the curtain seen from the
> outside. It is a fixed camera shot. Now we hear

the struggling heartbeat. Infinitely quiet, the closing music starts. It follows the rhythm of SELMA's irregular, fading pulse. It sounds like a phonograph record that can't decide on a single tempo. To this music we see images of SELMA from the film double-exposed onto our scene. Joyful images appear from what we have witnessed. Now the heart finally burns out. With one last strained beat, it ceases. So does the music. All is silent. The camera moves back now and cranes up and out into the night through the roof. All is black.

THE FILMFOUR BOOK OF FILM QUOTES

FILMFOUR Books presents a groovy guide to the best quotes from the movies; from mainstream blockbusters to cult classics; from the villain's final words to the leading lady's seductive speech.

In addition to famous quotes and the revealing of popular misquotes, the FILMFOUR Book also includes full-colour film stills.

• • •

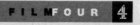